THE
Archive Photographs
SERIES

NEWPORT PEM
AND FISHGUARD

Coat of Arms of the Ancient Borough of Newport in the County of Pembrokeshire.

In the year 1090 family circumstances dictated that Robert Fitzmartin had to make a living outside the lands owned by his family in south-west England. He came to the hundred of Cemais which had its headquarters at Nevern. His grandson, William Fitzmartin married the daughter of Lord Rhys, who, unfortunately for William, had territorial aspirations which led to him ousting control of Cemais from the Fitzmartins. William subsequently established a garrison town overlooking the River Nevern estuary at Newport. This also provided him with sea communications. William christened his son after himself, and it was this William Fitzmartin who granted Newport its Charter in the year 1240. This gave the Burgesses of Newport certain rights and privileges within the town and it is from their number that the town's Mayor is elected annually. The Burgesses still meet at the Court Leet - a body of men dedicated to protecting their ancient rights, privileges, practices and traditions.

THE
Archive Photographs
SERIES

NEWPORT PEM
AND FISHGUARD

Compiled by
Martin Lewis

CHALFORD

First published 1996
Copyright © Martin Lewis, 1996

The Chalford Publishing Company
St Mary's Mill, Chalford,
Stroud, Gloucestershire, GL6 8NX

ISBN 0 7524 0637 X

Typesetting and origination by
The Chalford Publishing Company
Printed in Great Britain by
Redwood Books, Trowbridge

Also published in The *Archive Photographs* series
Saundersfoot and Tenby (Ken Daniels, 1995)
Pembrokeshire Returns (Ken Daniels, 1996)

Long Street, c. 1910. Mr Rowlands' bakery is on the left hand side (just out of shot). The three houses on the right form Bank Terrace with the Tabernacl Calvinistic Methodist Chapel (built 1815) just beyond.

Class 4 at Newport Pem. Council School, c. 1905. The children in this photograph include Eaton Vaughan (front left) and Hubut Phillips (front cover). Three of the girls in the back row are recorded simply as 'gypsy girls'.

Contents

Foreword

It gives me great pleasure to write a brief foreword to Mr Martin Lewis' book. I know that he has spoken to a number of organisations in the area on the subject of 'history on your door-step' and also that he has prepared this volume in direct response to the many requests that he has received.

It is often said that, second only to bereavement and divorce, moving house is the most stressful of activities in which one can indulge. Looking on the positive side, however, it is not without its excitement. Moving to a new area represents a voyage of discovery - discovering new and interesting people; discovering the history of your new locality and how it fitted into the overall scheme of things; discovering the history and significance of buildings in the area - the list is endless. All these things take time of course, but how much easier it is when there are publications written which provide some guidance on the subject.

Mr Lewis has gone a long way towards satisfying this need. He has presented a delightful collection of postcards, photographs and ephemera of the area, the like of which I have not previously seen in a private collection. I know also that those images included in this book represent only a small proportion of his collection, and that it has not been possible for him to include all that he would have wished in this book. With each image, he has given us just a little narrative, but sufficient to provide clear evidence of the extensive research which he has undertaken. This has not been easy because, as far as I am aware, there is relatively little printed material on the recent history of these communities. He has presented it in a most entertaining way and, like a good roast lunch, has left us feeling that we could do with a little more.

For me, the book is doubly pleasing in so far that he has included much that had to do with that most exciting of Great Western Railway projects - the building of Fishguard Harbour. We can all speculate on 'what might have been' - a transatlantic port on our doorstep, cargo boats to all parts of the globe, oil refineries at Goodwick, crack railway expresses to London and the Continent, let alone the economic and cultural changes which such developments would have brought.

The book is entertaining and light-hearted, the images are endlessly fascinating, and the narrative is a good read. It gives me great pleasure to commend the book to you.

Sir Lincoln Hallinan
Patron & Former President,
Victorian Society (South Wales Branch)
Deputy Lieutenant, County of South Glamorgan

East Street, c. 1906. Havard's Ironmongery Stores was established in 1840 and has been run by a member of the family ever since. The proprietor, John Llewellyn Havard (wearing a boater), poses here with staff and townsfolk while Mrs Havard stands at the entrance to the shop. The smart young lady (centre right) was Miss Mary Ann Howells who later married Captain Thomas Griffiths (see page 50a).

Introduction

I was attending a Philatelic Society Annual General Meeting c. 1987 where there were a small number of dealers in attendance. I had completed several 'laps' through their stock searching for material which, even if I had found, I would not have been able to afford, but I persevered for the want of anything better to do. I had always resisted the temptation to collect cigarette cards or coins - my history master had taught me that army generals who opened battle fronts that were too many or too long, always lost their wars; after all, look what happened to Hitler. I did, however, allow myself to look through a box of somewhat nondescript looking postcards (if there are such things), and, lo and behold, I stumbled across a card of the Parrog at Newport Pem. - my home town - published around 1930. Despite the teachings of my history master, I invested. For a modest 50p, this was an opportunity too good to miss. I pored over my new found treasure, and the instant I arrived home, the magnifying glass revealed a wealth of detail which I had never before been aware of. My dear mother, now in her eighty-third year, confirmed the visual detail and a host of other interesting facts about the area. Thus was my interest in postcards, old photographs and ephemera born.

Since that time, my collection of postcards of Newport Pem., Fishguard and Goodwick has grown to more than 1,600 and it is from this collection that all images in this book have been taken. It has thus been a difficult task to choose a suitable selection for this book. The problem has been largely one of what to leave out rather than what to include. Dates to each picture have been inserted, wherever possible, but when post-marked dates have been included, it is important to realise that the image on which the card is based may have been photographed several years earlier.

I was born in Newport Pem. but moved to Fishguard at an early age. My formative years were spent in these two towns, and they thus hold a very high place in my affections. This book is intended to represent a journey from Eglwyswrw in the north to Strumble Head in the west. It attempts to take a brief glimpse at social and economic activities of the area. It notes many of the local characters, important events which took place, and I hope it will, therefore, be of interest not only to the inhabitants of North Pembrokeshire, but also to the many visitors who spend holidays in this beautiful part of the country.

Due to constraints of space, it has not been possible to make mention of some aspects of the life of these communities. For example, the ship-building industry of Newport has not been mentioned other than in this introduction and other omissions include historical aspects of Newport and Nevern castles, the development of schools in the area (in particular, Fishguard County School) and the Court Leet at Newport.

The work, therefore, makes no pretence to be an exhaustive treatise on the recent history of these towns. It is hoped, nonetheless, that, within this social glimpse, readers will find the photographs of interest and the script enjoyable.

L. Martin 'Lewis'

Martin Lewis
"Nythfa", West Street
Newport, Pembrokeshire SA42 0TD

Bridge Street, c. 1923. Mr Thomas, the proprietor of the Commercial (now the Castle) Hotel, proudly displays his new 23 hp Ford while his wife and daughter stand along side. The gentleman wearing the bowler hat was Mr E.J. Griffiths of Trewern (see page 21).

One
Newport's
Surrounding Villages

Banc Uchaf, Eglwyswrw, c. 1925. Inhabitants of the village pose for the photograph, while the menfolk in the distance admire the two cars parked side by side across the road.

Banc Uchaf, Eglwyswrw, c. 1905. Road traffic of the day comprised only of the horse-drawn trap and the geese at the bottom of the hill.

Eglwyswrw - S 1602 M

Banc Isaf, Eglwyswrw (postmarked 1910) showing the dominant position of the church and the school within the village.

Rural District of St. Dogmeils

ELECTION

OF

RURAL DISTRICT

COUNCILLORS

IN THE YEAR 1904.

PARISH OF

EGLWYSWRW

NOTICE IS HEREBY GIVEN,

1.—That a Poll for the Election of Rural L... Councillors for the above-named Parish will be held on **Tuesday,** the **29th** day of **March, 1904,** between the hours of Two and Eight in the Afternoon.

2.—That the number of Rural District Councillors to be elected for the Parish is Two.

3.— That the names in alphabetical order, places of abode, and descriptions of the Candidates for election, and the names of their respective Proposers and Seconders, are as follows :—

Names of Candidate (Surname first).	Place of Abode.	Description.	Names of Proposer. (Surname first).	Names of Seconder. (Surname first).
Bowen, Thomas Davies	Penycoed ...	... Farmer	Thomas, Jonathan	... James, Samuel
Edwards, David John ...	Glandwrganol	... Farmer	Jenkins, John...	... James, Benjamin
Evans, William ...	Palle Farm	... Farmer	Harries, John ...	... Rees, John
Morgans, George ...	Nantyrhelygenfawr	Farmer	James, Benjamin	... Rees, Dan

4.—The situation of the Polling Place and Polling Station is as follows :—

THE BOARD SCHOOL, EGLWYSWRW.

5.—The Poll will be taken by Ballot, and the colour of the ordinary Ballot Paper used in the Election will be White.

Dated this 15th day of March, 1904.

DAVID DAVIES,

25, Quay Street, Cardigan.

RETURNING OFFICER.

J. C. ROBERTS, PRINTER, "OBSERVER" OFFICE, CARDIGAN.

A local elections poster from 1904.

The College, Felindre as it stands today. It was built by George Owen of Henllys to provide education for his own children and those in the community. It is known to have existed in 1594 when the headmaster was one Lewys Thomas, Bachelor of Arts. By the year 1601, however, he had taken holy orders and become Rector of Newport.

By 1739, the building had become an inn. It is also known that, on occasions, the Court Leet of the Barony of Cemais met here (see page 2). The detail above the door also indicates that, from 1552 to 1620, it was used as a courthouse.

The weir, Felindre, c. 1952. This was built c. 1900 to divert water to the mill (felin) which was used to crush grain. The water 'cascades' are to allow migratory fish (salmon and sewin) to travel up and down the river for spawning purposes.

The Salutation Inn, Felindre. A copy of the *Cardigan & Tivyside Advertiser* (15 June 1934) reads: 'The death took place on Sunday of a very well known and popular North Pembrokeshire personality, Mrs Elizabeth Lloyd of the Salutation Inn, Velindre, Nevern in her 91st year. The late Mrs Lloyd, who buried her husband twenty years ago, was born at the Salutation Inn and slept in the very room in which she was born. All her children predeceased her. Blessed with a retentive memory, Mrs Lloyd could tell many tales of the old coach days when the Salutation used to be the changing place for horses for the coach running between Cardigan and Fishguard'.

Nevern village, c. 1950. Nevern School stands on the right of this picture. The white house was the residence provided for the headmaster of the school. It shields from view the village post office.

The River Nevern, c. 1910. The girls on the wall are less adventurous than the boys in the river. The gentleman on the extreme right is thought to be Mr Davy Owen, a local tailor, with his daughter Megan.

14

Nevern School, c. 1896. The boys of the school pose for the camera under the watchful eye of the Headmaster, Mr Ward and teacher, Miss Hannah Davies. Mr Ward was a strong exponent of the 'Welsh Knot' whereby the last pupil to be caught speaking Welsh on any day would be required to wear the 'knot' around his/her neck and subsequently be caned the following morning.

Nevern School, 1925. About two years before this photograph was taken, Mr Ward was replaced by Mr W.J. Edwards who was to serve as Headmaster for more than twenty-five years. Miss Hannah Davies (left) is still in post after about thirty years service.

OCCUPIERS LIST OF VOTERS.

PARISH OF NEVERN (PEM.).

LIST OF THE PERSONS entitled to be Registered as Parliamentary Voters for the NEWPORT Polling Division, of the County of Pembroke, in respect of the Inhabitant Occupation of a Dwelling-house, or of the Occupation of any Land or Tenement of a clear Yearly Value of Ten Pounds, or of any right reserved by Section 10 of the Representation of the People Act, 1884, when such Dwelling-house, Land or Tenement is situate wholly or partly within this Parish, and the Persons entitled to be Registered as County Electors for the Administrative County of Pembroke, in respect of the Occupation of Property situate wholly or partly within this Parish.

DIVISION I.—Persons entitled to be Registered in respect of the Occupation aforesaid both as Parliamentary Electors and as County Electors.

Names of Voters in full, Surname being first.	Place of Abode.	Nature of Qualification.	Description of Qualifying Property.
Bowen, James Bevan	Llwyngwair	land and tenement	Llwyngwair
Bowen, Benjamin	Tirteg	dwelling house	Tirteg
Bowen, David	Sinar	dwelling house	Sinar
Bowen, John	Ty'riet	land and tenement	Ty'riet
Bowen, John	Pantyrhyg	dwelling house	Pantyrhyg
Davies, William	Penbont, Nevern	dwelling house	Penbont, Nevern
Daniel, John	Morfa-isaf	land and tenement, joint	Morfa-isaf
Daniel, Thomas	Morfa-isaf	land and tenement, joint	Morfa-isaf
Davies, James	Eisteddfa-fawr	land and tenement	Eisteddfa-fawr
Davies, David	Llwynihirion	land and tenement	Llwynihirion
Davies, William	Pontclydach	dwelling house	Pontclydach
Daniel, Thomas	Trewern Arms, Nevern	land and tenement	Trewern Arms
Davies, William	Ietgoch	dwelling house	Ietgoch
Daniel, William	Coedcadw	land and tenement	Coedcadw
Davies, Thomas	Bridgend Inn, Cilgwyn	dwelling house	Bridgend Inn
Davies, John	Bankybryn Smithy	dwelling house	Bankybryn Smithy
Davies, James	Gethsemane	dwelling house	Gethsemane
Davies, Daniel	Gernos	land and tenement	Gernos
Davies, William	Pistill	dwelling house	Pistill
Devonald, Thomas	Fagwrlwyd	land and tenement	Fagwrlwyd
Davies, George	Tynewydd, Morfa	dwelling house	Tynewydd
Davies, Dan	Penlan-isaf	land and tenement	Penlan-isaf and Penlan-uchaf
Davies, Stephen	Penlan-fach	dwelling house	Penlan-fach
Davies, John	Cilgwyn Mill	land and tenement	Cilgwyn Mill
Davies, John	Waunfach Smithy	dwelling house	Waunfach Smithy
Davies, David	Henfelin	dwelling house	Henfelin
Davies, David	Penant-du	land and tenement	Penant-du
Evans, William	Tredwr-isaf	dwelling house	Tredwr-isaf
Evans, John	Glasdir	land and tenement	Glasdir
Evans, William	Eisteddfa Arthur	land and tenement	Eisteddfa Arthur
Edwards, Benjamin	Tyllwyd	dwelling house	Tyllwyd
Evans, John	Tredwr	land and tenement	Tredwr
Evans, Joseph	Mynydd-du	land and tenement	Mynydd-du
Evans, Daniel	Cilwen	land and tenement	Ffynonias
Edwards, Warriet	Pantybroga	dwelling house	Pantybroga
Evans, John	Shop-fach	dwelling house	Shopfach
Edwards, Thomas	Ietwen	dwelling house	Ietwen
Edwards, John	Trewenfron-fawr	land and tenement	Trewenfron-fawr
Evans, Rees	Bwlchyfedwen	dwelling house, successive	Bwlchyfedwen and Bayvil
Evans, Ebenezer	Gamallt	land and tenement	Gamallt
Evans, Thomas	Eisteddfa Arthur	land and tenement, joint	Eisteddfa Arthur
Evans, James	Rhydyffeiriad	dwelling house	Rhydyffeiriad
Francis, John	Nantyclyn	land and tenement	Nantyclyn

PARISH OF NEVERN (PEM.) Continued.

Names of Voters in full, Surname being first.	Place of Abode.	Nature of Qualification.	Description of Qualifying Property
Griffiths, John	Bwlchyfedwen	dwelling house	Bwlchyfedwen
Griffiths, Thomas	Berry Lodge	dwelling house	Berry Lodge
Griffiths, Lewis	Ty'rfeidir	dwelling house	Ty'rfeidir
Griffiths, William	Pontclydach	dwelling house	Pontclydach
Gibby, Jabez	Tynewydd	dwelling house	Tynewydd
Gilbert, Llewelyn	Llystyn	land and tenement	Llystyn
Griffiths, David	Buarthgwyn	dwelling house	Buarthgwyn
George, Thomas	Henllys	land and tenement	Henllys
George, David	Danyrallt, Nevern	dwelling house	Danyrallt, Nevern
Griffiths, Thomas	Penlan-tafarn	dwelling house	Penlan-tafarn
Griffiths, David	Castellygynen	land and tenement	Castellygynen and Tyisaf
Griffiths, William	Wenallt	land and tenement	Wenallt
Griffiths, James	Ysguborwen	land and tenement	Ysguborwen
Griffiths, Jacob	Nantyclyn	dwelling house	Nantyclyn
Griffiths, John	Clynhenllan-uchaf, Cilgerran	land	Young's land
Griffiths, John	Tynewydd	dwelling house	Tynewydd
Griffiths, David	College	dwelling house	College
Harries, James	Gernos-fach	land and tenement	Gernos-fach
Harries, Owen	Pandy	dwelling house	Pandy
Harries, John	Ffynonwen	land and tenement	Ffynonwen
Harries, John	Gelly	land and tenement, joint	Gelly
Harries, Watkin	Gelly	land and tenement, joint	Gelly
Harries, Simon	Penparke	land and tenement	Penparke
Howells, John	Cilgwyn-mawr	land and tenement	Cilgwyn-mawr
Havard, Eynon	Crugiau	land and tenement, joint	Crugiau
Havard, William	Crugiau	land and tenement, joint	Crugiau
Harries, William	Prengast, Nevern	dwelling house	Prengast
Howells, John	Penfeidir	land and tenement	Penfeidir
Howells, Thomas	Esgerwen	land and tenement	Esgerwen
Howells, William	Nantsue	land and tenement	Nantsue
Howells, David	Pencnwc	land and tenement	Pencnwc
Howells, John	Trefach	land and tenement	Trefach
Hugh, John	Fachongle-ganol	land and tenement	Fachongle-ganol
Harries, David	Gelly	land and tenement, joint	Gelly
Harries, Joshua	Castellcadw	dwelling house	Castellcadw
Havard, Walter	Crugiau	land and tenement, joint	Crugiau
James, William	Morfa-mawr	land and tenement	Morfa-mawr
James, Evan	Pantymansel	dwelling house	Pantymansel
James, John	Court, Nevern	dwelling house	Court, Nevern
Jenkins, John	Fachongle-uchaf	land and tenement	Fachongle-uchaf
Jenkins, William	Llwynwhiod	dwelling house	Llwynwhiod
Jones, Samuel	Trefach, Morfa	land and tenement	Trefach
James, Owen	Pwllmarl	dwelling house	Pwllmarl
James, William	Rhoswrdan	land and tenement	Rhoswrdan
James, William	Carding Mill, Bryn	dwelling house	Carding Mill
James, Thomas	Bankrhyd-fawr	dwelling house	Banhrhyd-fawr
Jones, Thomas	Soar	dwelling house	Soar
Jenkins, Thomas	Glanrhyd	dwelling house	Glanrhyd
Jones, John	Spite	dwelling house	Spite
Jenkins, James	Berry Hill	dwelling house	Berry Hill
Jones, Thomas	Parke	dwelling house	Parke
James, David	Penlanwynt	land and tenement	Penlanwynt
James, William	Pencnwc, Morfa	dwelling house	Pencnwc
John, Joseph	Troedyrhiw	dwelling house	Troedyrhiw
Jones, Isaac Hughes	Nevern Vicarage	dwelling house	Nevern Vicarage
James, David	Trehaidd	land and tenement	Trehaidd
Jenkins, Evan Peregrine	Rhosfarket	land and tenement	Rhosfarket
James, Daniel	Tyrhibyn	dwelling house	Tyrhibyn
James, Thomas	Ffynonddofn	land and tenement	Ffynonddofn
James, Enoch	Clynery	dwelling house	Clynery
James, Thomas	Trefwrdan-isaf	land and tenement	Frefwrdan-isaf

Electoral list for the parish of Nevern in 1890. It will be noted that the list comprises men only - a total of 206. Men who owned land or property were entitled to vote in both Parliamentary and County elections.

PARISH OF NEVERN (PEM.) Continued.

Names of Voters in full, Surname being first.	Place of Abode.	Nature of Qualification.	Description of Qualifying Property.
Lewis, Evan	Blaenymeini	land and tenement	Blaenymeini
Lewis, Thomas	Dole, Nevern	dwelling house	Dole, Nevern
Lewis, William	Fronogwydd	dwelling house	Fronogwydd
Lewis, Watkin	Tynewydd	land and tenement	Tynewydd
Lewis, Evan	Iscoed	dwelling house	Iscoed
Llewelyn, James	Llwynbedw	dwelling house	Llwynbedw
Lloyd, John	Salutation Inn, Bayvil	land	Mill Meadows
Lewis, John	Penfeidir, Pencrugiau	land and tenement	Penfeidir
Lamb, Thomas	Tredryssi-fach	land and tenement	Tredryssi-fach
Lloyd, John	Taibach	dwelling house	Taibach
Lewis, Thomas	Plasparke	dwelling house	Plasparke
Lewis, John	Garfeth	land and tenement	Garfeth
Martin, John	Pen'rallt-walteried	land and tenement	Pen'rallt-walteried
Morris, John	Tymawr, Bryn	dwelling house	Tymawr, Bryn
Mathias, John	Llwyngwair Lodge	dwelling house	Llwyngwair Lodge
Morgan, John	Pwll	land and tenement, joint	Pwll
Morgan, Thomas	Pwll	land and tenement, joint	Pwll
Morgan, David	Pen'rallt, Nevern	land and tenement	Pen'rallt, Nevern
Morris, William	Glasdir-bach	dwelling house	Glasdir-bach
Morris, David	Alltycwmins	dwelling house	Alltycwmins
Morris, Jacob	Bronydd	land and tenement	Bronydd
Morris, Roger	Rhydiau	dwelling house	Rhydiau
Morris, William	Bwlchyfedwen	dwelling house	Bwlchyfedwen
Marsden, John	Rhydyberw	dwelling house	Rhydyberw
Miles, Griffith Thomas	Cross Roads Schoolhouse	dwelling house	Cross Roads Schoolhouse
Morris, William	Pen'ralltygardde	land and tenement	Pen'ralltygardde
Nicholas, Morris	Penlan, Pencrugiau	dwelling house	Penlan
Nicholas, John	Tyrhos	dwelling house	Tyrhos
Nicholas, Morris	Pen'ralltgoch	dwelling house	Pen'ralltgoch
Nicholas, Thomas	College Mill, Bayvil	land	College Fields
Nicholas, Thomas	Ffosmarch	dwelling house	Ffosmarch
Nicholas, David	Rhosfach	dwelling house	Rhosfach
Owen, William Harries	Frongoch	land and tenement, joint	Frongoch
Owen, Owen	Frongoch	land and tenement, joint	Frongoch
Owen, John	Pwllybroga	dwelling house	Pwllybroga
Owen, Evan	Trefach Mill	land and mill	Trefach Mill
Owen, William	Pwllybroga, Cilgwyn	dwelling house	Pwllybroga, Cilgwyn
Owen, William	Penwaunhir	dwelling house	Penwaunhir
Owen, Simon	Penant-du-uchaf	land and tenement, successive	Penant-du-uchaf and Penbank
Phillips, John	Glandwr	land and tenement	Glandwr
Phillips, Ebenezer	Glanafon	dwelling house	Glanafon
Phillips, John	Postcoch Smithy	dwelling house	Postcoch Smithy
Pritchard, Hugh	Tyllosg	land and tenement	Tyllosg
Phillips, William	Taibach, Penwern	dwelling house	Taibach
Phillips, Richard	Quarrel	dwelling house	Quarrel
Richards, Joshua	Cwmins-bach, Meline	land	Pantyrodyn
Rees, David	Dolbont	land and tenement	Dolbont
Rees, Lewis	Cilwen	land and tenement	Cilwen
Rees, William	Tyrbwlch	land and tenement	Tyrbwlch
Rees, James	Tyrbwlch	dwelling house	Tyrbwlch
Rees, Benjamin	Tycanol	land and tenement	Tycanol
Richards, John	Ivybush, Nevern	dwelling house	Ivybush, Nevern
Richards, David	Cwmgloyne	land and tenement	Cwmgloyne
Rowe, John	Cwmcene	land and tenement, joint	Cwmcene
Rowe, Lewis	Cwmcene	land and tenement, joint	Cwmcene
Rowlands, John	Argoed	land and tenement	Argoed
Rees, Thomas	Mount Pleasant	dwelling house	Mount Pleasant
Rees, Joseph	Waunbwl	dwelling house	Part of Plasybedde
Richards, Daniel	Rhydymane	land and tenement	Rhydymane

PARISH OF NEVERN (PEM.) Continued.

Names of Voters in full, Surname being first.	Place of Abode.	Nature of Qualification.	Description of Qualifying Proper
Selby, John	Plasyffynon	land and tenement	Plasyffynon
Thomas, John	Plasybank	land and tenement	Plasybank
Thomas, William	Pengwndwn-bach	dwelling house	Pengwndwn-bach
Thomas, Benjamin	Penfeidir	land and tenement	Penfeidir
Thomas, James	Penbenglog Mill	dwelling house	Penbenglog Mill
Thomas, Thomas	Pontbren	dwelling house	Pontbren
Thomas, David	Tyrhibyn	dwelling house	Tyrhibyn
Thomas, John	Start	dwelling house	Start
Thomas, David	Fachongle-isaf	land and tenement	Fachongle-isaf
Thomas, Titus	Tyrffynon	dwelling house	Tyrffynon
Thomas, John	Frosty Hill	dwelling house	Frosty Hill
Thomas, William	Samaria	dwelling house	Samaria
Thomas, Thomas	Tygwyn	land and tenement	Tygwyn
Thomas, Owen Lloyd	Glanyrafon	dwelling house	Glanyrafon
Thomas, William	Pontybaldan	dwelling house	Pontybaldan
Thomas, Joshua	Mountain Hall	land and tenement	Mountain Hall
Thomas, John	Tophill	dwelling house	Tophill
Thomas, James	Pengwndwn	dwelling house	Pengwndwn
Trollip, Jacob	Cardigan	land and tenement	Trellyffaint
Thomas, David	Tygwyn	land and tenement	Tygwyn
Thomas, David	Clyncoch	dwelling house	Clyncoch
Thomas Thomas	Coedwinog-fach	dwelling house	Coedwinog-fach
Thomas, Thomas	Dolbont Carding Mill	dwelling house	Dolbont Carding Mill
Vaughan, John	Clynyrwyn	land and tenement, joint	Clynyrwyn
Vaughan, David	Clynyrwyn	land and tenement, joint	Clynyrwyn
Volk, David	Castellygarn	land and tenement	Castellygarn
Volk, Thomas	Pentrissillt	land and tenement, joint	Pentrissillt
Vaughan, John	Tregynon	land and tenement	Tregynon
Vaughan, Benjamin	Pen'ralltddu	land and tenement	Pen'ralltddu
Vaughan, Benjamin	Trefwrdan-uchaf	land and tenement	Trefwrdan-uchaf
Williams, John	Penwernddu	land and tenement	Penwernddu
Ward, Alfred	Chapel House, Nevern	dwelling house	Chapel House
Williams, William	Rhosmaen	land and tenement	Rhosmaen
Williams, John	Pantry	dwelling house	Pantry
Williams, William	Ietgoch	dwelling house	Ietgoch
Williams, William	Pen'rallt-fach	dwelling house	Pen'rallt-fach
Williams, John	Castle Green	dwelling house	Castle Green
Williams, Thomas	Penwaun	dwelling house	Penwaun
Williams, David	Prengast	dwelling house	Prengast
Williams, John	Tafarnbwlch	land and tenement	Tafarnbwlch
Williams, Thomas	Shopfach	dwelling house	Shopfach
Williams, Thomas	Pontnewydd	dwelling house	Pontnewydd
Williams, John	Penbank	dwelling house, successive	Penbank & Clyndwn, White

Dated this 31st day of July, in the year One thousand eight hundred and ninety.

Overseers of the Pa
of Nevern (Pen

J. C. ROBERTS, PRINTER, "OBSERVER" OFFICE, CARDIGAN.

Electoral list (ladies) for the parish of Nevern in 1890: ladies were allowed to vote in County elections only. Their list comprises only 65 names.

OCCUPIERS LIST OF VOTERS.

PARISH OF NEVERN (PEM.).

LIST OF THE PERSONS entitled to be Registered as Parliamentary Voters for the NEWPORT Polling Division, of the County of Pembroke, in respect of the Inhabitant Occupation of a Dwelling-house, or of the Occupation of any Land or Tenement of a clear Yearly Value of Ten Pounds, or of any right reserved by Section 10 of the Representation of the People Act, 1884, when such Dwelling-house, Land or Tenement is situate wholly or partly within this Parish, and the Persons entitled to be Registered as County Electors for the Administrative County of Pembroke, in respect of the Occupation of Property situate wholly or partly within this Parish.

LADIES' LIST.

DIVISION III.—Persons entitled to be Registered in respect of the Occupation aforesaid as County Electors but not as Parliamentary Electors.

Names of Voters in full, Surname being first.	Place of Abode.	Nature of Qualification.	Description of Qualifying Property.
Bowen, Mary	Pengawse	dwelling house	Pengawse
Davies, Elizabeth	Noble Court	dwelling house	Noble Court
Davies, Elizabeth	Llwynbedw	dwelling house	Llwynbedw
Davies, Anne	Badger	dwelling house	Badger
Davies, Anne	Blaencwm, Llanerch	dwelling house	Blaencwm
Davies, Grace	Llwyngores	land and tenement, joint	Llwyngores
Davies, Jane	Llwyngores	land and tenement, joint	Llwyngores
Davies, Martha	Coedwinog	land and tenement	Coedwinog
Davies, Margaret	Cnwcyllydy	land and tenement	Cnwcyllydy
Daniel, Elizabeth	Morfa-isaf	land and tenement, joint	Morfa-isaf
Edwards, Mary Anne	Brenkin	dwelling house	Brenkin
Evans, Mary	Treicert	land and tenement	Treicert
Evans, Mary	Tanerdy	dwelling house	Tanerdy
Evans, Margaret	Pencnwc, Crugiau	land and tenement	Pencnwc, Crugiau
Francis, Mary	Castellyglonc	dwelling house	Castellyglonc
Griffiths, Elizabeth	Square and Compass	dwelling house	Square and Compass
Griffiths, Mary	Tredryssi-fawr	land and tenement	Tredryssi-fawr
George, Hannah	Pontybaldan	dwelling house	Pontybaldan
Howells, Eleanor	Pwll-llaca	dwelling house	Pwll-llaca
Havard, Ellen	Crugian	land and tenement, joint	Crugian
Harries, Elizabeth	Gelly	land and tenement, joint	Gelly
Jones, Anne	Penbwcle	dwelling house	Penbwcle
Jones, Mary	Lookabout	dwelling house	Lookabout
John, Anne	Dolbont Cottage	dwelling house	Dolbont Cottage
James, Anne	Gwerngwyddil	dwelling house	Gwerngwyddil
James, Hannah	Danybank	dwelling house	Danybank
Jones, Mary	Bankybryn	dwelling house	Bankybryn
James, Mary	Ffynonias-isaf	dwelling house	Ffynonias-isaf
James, Martha	Parkyscos	dwelling house	Parkyscos
James, Elizabeth	Penwaun	dwelling house	Penwaun
Jones, Margaret	Pontgareg	dwelling house	Pontgareg
James, Lettice	Pentop	dwelling house	Pentop
James, Jestina	Greenland, Bryn	dwelling house	Greenland, Bryn
Jenkins, Leah	Plasybancor	dwelling house	Plasybancor
James, Hannah	Storehouse	dwelling house	Storehouse
James, Martha	Tyrhibyn	dwelling house	Tyrhibyn
Laugharne, Catherine	Cwm	dwelling house	Cwm

PARISH OF NEVERN (PEM.) Continued.

Names of Voters in full, Surname being first.	Place of Abode.	Nature of Qualification.	Description of Qualifying Property.
Lewis, Mary	Quarrel	dwelling house	Quarrel
Lloyd, Mary	Temple Bar	land and tenement	Temple Bar
Lewis, Mary	Penbont	dwelling house	Penbont
Lewis, Elizabeth	Penbont, Cilgwyn	dwelling house	Penbont, Cilgwyn
Lloyd, Phoebe	Penbig	dwelling house	Penbig
Lloyd, Jane	Plasyberth	dwelling house	Plasyberth
Lloyd, Sarah	Fronwen	dwelling house	Fronwen
Morris, Martha	Ddolgam	dwelling house	Ddolgam
Morgan, Anne	Plasybedde	land and tenement	Plasybedde
Morgan, Mary	Pen'rallt, Nevern	land and tenement, joint	Pen'rallt, Nevern
Morgan, Rachel	Llystyn-isaf	dwelling house	Llystyn-isaf
Morris, Ruth	Bankybryn	dwelling house	Bankybryn
Phillips, Anna	Dole, Nevern	dwelling house	Dole, Nevern
Phillips, Anne	Pantyrodyn	dwelling house	Pantyrodyn
Rees, Anne	Pentre Evan	land and tenement	Pentre Evan
Rees, Hannah	Tregaman	land and tenement	Tregaman
Rees, Maria	Waunbwl	dwelling house	Waunbwl
Rees, Elizabeth	Tycanol	land and tenement, joint	Tycanol
Stephens, Margaret	Penllyn	dwelling house	Penllyn
Thomas, Mary	Bankybryn	dwelling house	Bankybryn
Thomas, Esther	Trewenfron	land and tenement	Trewenfron
Thomas, Margaret	Taibach, Penwern	dwelling house	Taibach
Vaughan, Maria	Ffynondicky	land and tenement	Ffynondicky
Watkins, Martha	Cwmeog	land and tenement	Cwmeog
Williams, Martha	Crane Hill	dwelling house	Cranehill
Williams, Mary Anne	Penwern	land and tenement	Penwern
Williams, Anne	Penrhiwlas	dwelling house	Penrhiwlas
Williams, Hannah	Pontbren	dwelling house	Pontbren

Dated this 31st day of July, in the year One thousand eight hundred and ninety.

Overseers of the Parish
of Nevern (Pem).

St Brynach's Church, Nevern (postmarked 1909). It is said that Brynach settled on the banks of the Caman Brook to escape the attentions of a jealous woman and that he would commune with the angels at the summit of Carn Ingli - the mountain behind Newport. Apart from the church at Nevern, he established churches at Pontfaen (in the Gwaun Valley), Llanfyrnach and Llanboidy (Whitland). The church at Dinas is also dedicated to St Brynach.

The 'Mounting Steps' at Nevern. These are situated just outside the churchyard. A horse would be brought alongside, the lady would climb the steps, and thus be able to straddle her mount in a genteel and ladylike manner.

The Celtic cross, Nevern churchyard. The stone is 24 inches wide and up to 18 inches thick, and stands about 13 feet above the ground. The intricate patterns carved on it have, so far, defied interpretation. Legend has it that the first cuckoo to arrive in spring stands on this stone, and the singing of its song formally heralds the arrival of summer.

Advertising postcard from 1912. Although posters were prominently displayed (as they are today), the same information was often printed on postcards and distributed to parties who were thought to be interested. Such documents were generally stored on a curved 'wire' - hence the hole in the middle.

TREFACH
NEVERN.

A Large and Very Important Clear-Out Sale of Stock, Crops, Implements, and Household Furniture.

MR. D. HUGHES

Has been favoured with instructions from Mr. Jones to Sell by Public Auction, on

Tuesday, 8th of October, 1912,

THE FOLLOWING :—

CROPS: 200 Mows of Corn (Oats, Barley, and Mixed Corn), 1 Rick of Seed Hay, and 2 Stacks of Meadow Hay.

CATTLE: 55 Head of Cattle, viz., 16 Cows, 3 In-calf Heifers, 16 Yearling Steers & Heifers, 10 Forward Calves, 8 younger Calves, 1 Yearling Bull.

HORSES: 2 Aged Mares and 1 two-year-old Shire Filly.

PIGS: 1 Fat Sow, 1 Sow with Litter, 1 Sow lately farrowed.

ALL the IMPLEMENTS, HARNESS, DAIRY UTENSILS, and part of the HOUSEHOLD FURNITURE.

Credit on Conditions. Luncheon at 11. Sale at 12 prompt.

NOTE.—The Cattle are in exceptionally good condition, most of the Cows being young, very well-bred, and exceedingly good milkers.

The Auctioneer respectfully calls the attention of the public to this Important Sale, as Mr. Jones is giving up Farming, and therefore is disposing of all his Stock, &c.

PLEASE ATTEND PUNCTUALLY.

For further particulars see Posters.

Offices—Priory St., Cardigan, & Old Post Office, N.C. Emlyn, Attending at Newport & Eglwyswrw on Fair Days.

J. C. ROBERTS AND SON, PRINTERS, CARDIGAN.

Pentre Ifan Farm, Brynberian (postmarked 1911). Mr John Rees farmed the property for many years until his retirement c. 1930. He is seen here with his two sisters (dressed in black), along with other farm staff. The property has recently been acquired by the Welsh League of Youth (Urdd Gobaith Cymru).

Trewern Farm, Newport, 1936. Both Trewern and Pentre Ifan were considered as 'gentry houses' in their time. The recently widowed Mrs M.J. Griffiths is seen standing in the gateway with her daughter, Elizabeth Mary (Lit), and her prospective son-in-law, Mr William Lewis, on the day of their engagement.

The farmers of Trewern and Pentre Ifan, Messrs John Rees and Evan James Griffiths, were close friends. Mr Griffiths was sadly involved in a shooting accident, which ultimately led to his death. He was buried in 1935, on the day before his fiftieth birthday.

Mr Thomas Edward lived in a homestead called Bwlchmelyn, near Temple Bar. He was employed at Trewern Farm and drove a wagon drawn by two horses to distribute the malt produced at Trewern to local breweries, taverns and farms. After Thomas had enjoyed the hospitality offered by each establishment, the horses had little need of his driving skills for the return journey!

Brynberian Sunday school, c. 1910. The village of Brynberian at this time comprised of no more than about half a dozen houses, a post office and a chapel. The chapel, however, became the social centre for families living within about a five mile radius.

Pentre Ifan cromlech, thought to date from c. 3500 BC, comprises of a capstone some 16 feet in length supported by three standing stones. In his *Historical Tour through Pembrokeshire* (1903), the Fishguard historian, Richard Fenton, quotes the noted Elizabethan antiquarian of the county, George Owen, as saying: 'worth noting is the stone called Maen-y-Gromlech in Pentre-Jevan lande. It is a huge and massie stone mounted on high, and set on the topps of three other high stones pitched, standing upright in the ground, which far surpasseth for bignes and hight Arthur's stone in the way betweene Hereford and the Hay or, Llech-yr-Ast neere Blaenporth in Cardiganshire, or any other that ever I sawe; saving some in Stonehenge upon Salisburie Plain.... The stones whereon this is layd are soe high that a man on horseback may well ryde under it without stowping... the whole is more than twenty oxen could draw...'

One
Newport
Capital of the Barony

Castle, West View, Newport (Pem.).

Newport Castle, c. 1905. This castle was built by William Fitzmartin c. 1200 and for more than two centuries served as the home of the Lord Marcher of the Barony of Cemais, and also as headquarters of the Barony.

East Street, Newport, c. 1928. The first building on the right is the Llwyngwair Arms, where the Court Leet of the Barony of Cemais have met for many years (and still do). The second building on the right is known as the Sessions House. It is probably here that the following judgement, written in rather dense legalese, and poorly punctuated, was pronounced in the middle of the nineteenth century.

'BE IT REMEMBERED that on the second day of September in the year of our Lord one thousand, eight hundred and forty two at the Castle Inn in the Town and parish of Newport in the County of Pembroke MARIA LEWIS singlewoman is duly convicted before us John Pugh Clerk and John William Taubmann James Esquire of Her Majesty's Justices of the peace acting in and for the said County. For that she the said Maria Lewis on the sixth day of August in the year aforesaid, at the parish of Fishguard in the County aforesaid Two gallon measures of cultivated roots called Potatoes commonly used for the food of man, the property of Henry Collins, in certain land of the said Henry Collins there situate (not being a garden orchard or nursery ground) then and there growing, then and there in the said land unlawfully did damage with intent the same then and there unlawfully so steal take and carry away, thereby then and there doing injury to the said Henry Collins to the amount of seven pence against the form of the statute in that case made and provided.

We the said Justices do therefore adjudge the said Maria Lewis for her said offence to be imprisoned in the House of Correction of the County aforesaid, at Haverfordwest and there kept to hard labour for the space of one calendar month.

GIVEN under our hands and seals the day and year first above mentioned.'

23 June 1843

Market Street, Newport, c. 1906. This street was, and still is, the commercial centre of the town. It is interesting to note the availability of bananas at this early date.

Long Street, Newport, c. 1907. The horse-drawn vehicle, which is thought to have been the town omnibus plying to and from the harbour at the Parrog, has just arrived outside the Angel Temperance Hotel - known by many, to this day, as 'The Temperance'.

Parish of
Newport, Pembs
**Names of the men from this
Parish who served their
King & Country in the**
Great War 1914-18

Capt. Arthur Havard
Capt. George Bowen
Capt. John Bowen
Capt. Robert L.Phillips
Lieut. John Davies RNR
Lieut. Essex H.Havard RNR
Lieut. David G.Tudor
Sgt.Major W.Y.Davies
Sgt.Major Price Gibby
Sgt.Major Willie Evans
Sgt.Major R'land Daniel(K)
Lce.Cpl.George Jenkins
Lce.Cpl.Willie Evans
Lce.Cpl.Trevor Williams
Private Arthur Edwards
Private Willie James   (K)
Private Thos.J.Peregrine (K)
Private Charles P.Thomas
Private E.F.Drewitt   (K)
Lce.Cpl.Clifford Evans   (K)
Private W.B.Evans
          John Morgans RNR
Private Daniel Thomas   (D)
Private David Harries
Private Tom Rees
Private Victor Lewis
Lce.Cpl.Willie Thomas
Private Arthur Lewis
Private David Richards
Private David G. James
Private Hubert Davies
Private John David
Private George Owen
Private David Stephens
Lce.Cpl.Peter Johns
Private Willie Lewis
Private Edgar Jenkins

Private Tom Edwards
Private Thomas Thomas
Private William Ll.Rees
Private Arthur Nicholls
Private Johnny Howells
Private Harold Williams
Private Owen Davies
Private Willie Tudor
Private Ernest Lawrence (D)
Private Rowland Owen
Private Tom G. Davies
Private Donald Hoskiss
Private Herber Lloyd (K)
Private William Hoskiss
Private Danny James
Private Llewellyn R.John
Private David Vaughan (M)
Private Morgan Evans
Private Benjamin John
Private Tom Griffiths
Private Titus Lewis
Private John Selby
Private Tom Lewis
Private Eric Evans
Private Willie H.James
Private Tom Davies
Private James Morgan
Private Freddie W.John (M)
Private David R.Peregrine
Private Willie Stephens
Private Stephen Backshell
Private David Davies
Private Gwilym Davies
Private Llewellin Davies
Private Redwin James
Private Howard G.L.Phillips
Private James S.Morgan
Private John Davies

Private Joseph Williams
Private Thomas Bowen
Private Clifford Varney
Private Morris Phillips
Private Tom Miles
Private David Evans
Private David John
Private Tom Evans
Private James Williams
Private David Williams
Lt.Comr.B.William George
Private David W.Thomas(D)
Private Fred Webb
Private Tom James
Private John James
Private Willie Jenkins
Private Tom Thomas
Private Eric Isbester
Private Walter Thomas
Private Evan Harries
Seaman D.J.Nicholls RNR
Seaman John Nicholas RNR
Private Tom James
Sgt.   T.E.Jones
Private Willie Beynon
Private Tom John
Private Willie Harries
Captain Joseph Davies (K)
Captain David Davies   (K)
A.B.   Tom Varney   (K)
A.B.   Raymond Evans (K)
A.B.   William Edwards (K)
A.B.   David Owen   (K)
A.B.   Freddie Howells (K)
A.B.   John Davies   (K)
Engineer George Hughes(K)
Private T.J.Selby Davies

(K - Killed in Action)   (D - Died in Action)   (M - Missing in Action)

A copy of a framed plaque which currently hangs in St Mary's Church.

H.M.T. CAMERONIA
En charge à X...

HMT *Cameronia* (His Majesty's Troopship), c. 1915. During the First World War, the SS *Cameronia* was commandeered by HM Government. She was used as a troop carrier to carry the third battalion of the Royal Welch Fusiliers to Egypt. In April 1917, she was torpedoed off Malta. On board was Private Arthur Lewis (right) who wrote a graphic account of the sinking in a 32 verse poem which appeared in the *Fishguard County Echo* in August 1917.

Scoutmaster Arthur Lewis, c. 1910. Mr Lewis was a very active member of the community. He, along with his brother, Willie, became a stonemason within his father's business. Outside his work, and apart from his scouting activities, he played the cornet in the Newport Town Band, and acted in nearly all local dramatic society productions.

27

Mr Thomas Rowe Lewis' Sunday school class at St Mary's Church in May 1940. From left to right, front row: Mrs Thomas (Market Street); Miss Elsie Varney (behind); Mrs Dora Varney; Mrs Ernest Thomas; Mr Thomas Rowe Lewis; Miss Annie Davies; Mrs Harries (Blaenwaun); Mrs Craddock (West Street). Second row: Miss James (?); Miss James (Victoria Lodge); Mrs Mary Varney; Mrs Lloyd (School House); Miss Davies (Cross House). Back row: Revd Jeffrey Jones; Mrs Evans (Parc y Person); Miss James (Castle Street); Mr Willie Lewis (stonemason); Mrs Varney (Glantowy); Mrs Wylde; Miss Edith Lewis; Mr J.T. Isaac.

The Girls' Friendly Society was another group organised by St Mary's Church. Here they are seen on one of their regular visits to Traeth Mawr (the 'big beach'), c. 1935.

The British Women's Temperance Association pictured outside the Church Chapel, Upper St Mary's Street (c. 1912) during one of their St David's Day celebrations. The group were dedicated to reducing alcohol dependence and addiction, and succeeded in reducing the number of Newport's public houses from about twenty-seven (c. 1850) to a mere fourteen by the year 1895.

Newport Sports Committee, 1909. Front row, from left to right: Messrs Ernest Davies, -?-, H.R. Felix, Van Bowen (Chairman), Capt Mathias, Mr John Bowen and Mr G.B. Bowen. The other rows include Messrs Benjamin W. Taylor, Tom Evans, W. Thomas and Arthur Lewis.

Madame Bevan's Central School, Newport. Madame Bridget Bevan died in 1779 but left a large amount of money in her will for the development of education in the area. By 1811, schools existed in seven parishes. There were a total of 98 scholars at St Dogmaels, 220 at Nevern and 138 at Newport!

John Morgans, schoolmaster, who served at the Madame Bevan Central School for a period of 47 years. He died in 1865 aged 79, and is buried in Newport churchyard. He is commemorated by a stained glass window inside the church.

Newport County Primary School, Lower St Mary's Street, c. 1910. The school was established at these premises around 1875 where it remained for nearly 120 years. When it was transferred to new purpose-built premises at the bottom of Long Street in 1992, the above property was adapted for use as a business centre and youth hostel.

The staff of Newport County Primary School in 1928: Mrs Patti Lewis (née Davies), Mrs Enid Davies, Mr T.R. Davies (Headmaster), Mrs Peggy Baker (née Evans) and Mrs Gwladys Evans (née Jones). Mr Titus Lewis is at the top right of the picture.

Ffair Gurig, Newport Pem., c. 1910. This is the annual street fair held in the second half of June each year. Evidence exists of horse sales in West Street, donkey sales in Bridge Street (above) and pig sales in Market Street. Even to this day, Ffair Gurig is still held in Long Street in Newport in the middle of June.

The Court Leet of the Barony of Cemais which still meets three or four times each year. Here they are seen in the Remembrance Day procession to Ebeneser Chapel c. 1957. The procession is led by Mr William James (Mace-bearer), Mr Jeffrey George (Clerk to the Court), the Mayor and Mayoress, Alderman and Mrs George Evans, the Revd Ald. and Mrs L.G. Lewis, and Councillor Howard Roberts.

The visit of the Duchess of Kent to Newport in 1951. The young lady presenting the Duchess with a bunch of flowers is the daughter of the Mayor, Alderman Dilwyn Miles. Pictured, from left to right: Miss Bosville, Mr T.R. Davies (Headmaster), The Duchess, Councillor Howard Roberts, the Mayor, Mr William James (Mace-bearer), the Mayoress, -?-, Mr Jeffrey George (Clerk to the Court Leet).

The radio variety programme, *Have a Go* visits Newport on 10 February 1956. Being presented to Wilfred Pickles and 'Give him the money' Mabel after the show, from left to right: Mr Essex Havard, Mrs Margaret Mathias, Capt Johnny Davies, Mr Wilfred Pickles, Mable, Mrs Joyce Joy (with the corgi), -?- and Miss Marion Thomas.

Miss Vera Evans (daughter of Mr Tom Evans, Manchester House), poses by the watermill at Newport, c. 1910. She was later to marry Captain Morris John Morgan (see page 50b).

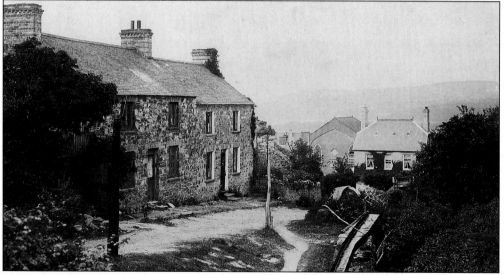

The mill at Newport, c. 1910. The watermill is here viewed from upstream. Micro examination of the original photograph reveals that a rope or wire stretched from the first floor of the woollen mill (left) to the wooden pole in the centre of the picture and thence to a 'flap' in the water duct. Activating the 'wire' would prevent the water from reaching the main drive of the wheel and thus stop it turning.

Plane crash at Carn Ffoi in 1934. A report written in the *Fishguard County Echo* on 19 August read: 'A crowd had gathered on the slopes of Carn Ffoi, Newport, Pem where an aeroplane had to make a forced landing at about 3.30 this morning. It was an Italian machine - bright red in hue. The occupants were said to be an American who received injuries and had to be taken to Cardigan Hospital, and an Italian who was much shaken, but on the whole they had a miraculous escape considering the machine had completely turned over. Mrs G. Slade, housekeeper to the Rev. Canon Phillips, said that she heard the machine go over the Rectory at about 2.45 am. It was flying very low, and although she knows nothing about machines, was quite sure all was not right'.

A letter carried by the crashed plane which the postmaster, Mr Tom Thomas (see page 55b), at the time very properly rescued from the scene of the crash. All such mail was franked at Newport prior to onward transmission.

Cambria Terrace, Newport Pem. (postmarked 1907). The post office is the last (white) house on the left of the street. The vehicles (centre right) are almost certainly the horse-drawn omnibus to Fishguard & Goodwick station, and the daily mail coach.

West Street, Newport Pem. (postmarked 1914). The second house on the left (with bay windows) was the town's police station until c. 1968. The house still bears the mark where the Pembrokeshire Police emblem was once mounted.

STATION *Newport.*

PARISHES COVERED *Newport.*
Nevern. Meline. Morvil

TEL. NO. *Newport 6. 1931*
SECTION *Fishguard / Eglwyswrw*
DIVISION *Fishguard*

FORMED			CEASED			REMARKS (including address)
9	8	1857	4	4	1977	Station closed down.
						New Station built

OFFICERS POSTED

FROM			TO			OFFICER	T/S	REMARKS
9	5	1857	2	11	1857	Pc.11. John Thomas		
2	11	1857	19	5	1858	Pc.14. John Jacob	T	from Landshipping
20	5	1858	20	6	1860	Pc.18 Edward Irving		
20	6	1860			1861	Pc.11. Michael Carroll.		
		1861			1869	APS.38 David Pearce.		
		1869	17	12	1879	Pc.12. James Symmonds.		
17	12	1879	18	10	1893	Pc.29. Jason Beynon.		
20	11	1893	30	9	1908	Pc.3 Josiah Morgan.		
30	9	1908	11	1	1922	Pc.32. David James		
11	1	1922	9	10	1933	Pc.50. Thos Morgan Owen	T	to Kilgerran.
9	10	1933	24	11	1937	Pc.27. Ben Williams		
24	11	1937	8	5	1946	Pc.39. Thos Owen Preece	T	to Mathry.
8	5	1946	29	4	1955	Pc.40 John Francis Thomas	Sgt	to Crymmych.
29	4	1955	17	5	1962	Pc.54 H Edward Phillips	T	to P.St.
17	5	1962	1	4	1968	Pc.125. David Williams		
			1	4	1968	Dyfed Powys Police		
7	4	1968				Pc.125 Dd Williams	T	to Penybontfawr
						Pc 80 Williams		
			4	4	1977	Pc 382 M. Rees. Station closed down		

Please see overleaf for NOTES.

The official record of all those police officers who served at Newport Pem. for more than a century (1857-1968). In January 1869 the following note appears in the record: 'APS [Acting Police Sergeant] 38 David Pearce. Using filthy language - called upon to resign... but at the request of the respectable inhabitants of Newport and others, who gave him a good character as an officer for a period of eight years, the resignation is allowed to be withdrawn'.

Councillor Howard Roberts on his motor cycle, c. 1918. With the reduction of maritime activities at Newport Pem., the town's mariners had to travel to Swansea or Cardiff in order to join ship. Recognising a need, Mr Roberts carried sailors to Fishguard & Goodwick Station on his motor cycle. The traffic became so brisk that it was not long before he had a side-car fitted.

'Gatehouse', West Street, Newport, c. 1932. Mr Jim Harries and his family lived here for many years. He ran a thriving business in shoe repairs from premises situated to the rear of the building. He is seen here with his wife and baby, Will, in the shawl. It was to this and an adjacent site that Councillor Roberts transferred the Pioneer Motor Bus Company from Parrog Road.

The first Pioneer motor bus, c. 1919. Councillor Roberts started to run the service from Fishguard to Cardigan at about this time, but it was not long before he was in fiery competition with a similar service offered by the Great Western Railway Company (GWR).

Road traffic accident outside Dewi Villa, Newport Pem. A report at the time read: 'On the morning of 19 August 1925, one of the company's (GWR's) AEC buses on its journey from Newport (Pem) to Fishguard and Goodwick Station collided with an opposition bus owned by Messrs. Roberts of Newport which was travelling in the opposite direction. Wheel hubs touched, and the GWR bus ended up on its side across the road, fortunately without injuring any passengers though they doubtless missed their train!'

The opening of the Memorial Hall, Newport Pem. The hall was officially opened on 26 September 1923. The interior of the programme (opposite) informs us that the order of procession was: (a) soldiers and sailors (above); (b) the Mayor and Lord Marcher (below); (c) the clergy and ministers; (d) the Corporation Court Leet; (e) the ladies' committee; (f) the schoolchildren.

Newport (Pem) Memorial Hall

Souvenir-Programme

—OF—

Opening Ceremony

—BY—

Sir MARTEINE O. M. LLOYD, Bart.,

Lord Marcher of the Barony of Kemes,

On Wednesday, September 26th, 1923,

AT 2 O'CLOCK.

Cover of the souvenir programme for the opening ceremony of the Newport Pem. Memorial Hall, 1923. After a brief service of dedication, short addresses were given by Major Gwilym Lloyd George MP; G.B. Bowen JP; J.O. Vaughan (ex Mayor); Dr D. Havard; David Luke; Sgt Major W. Young Davies; J.Ll. Havard; E.M. Davies; E.R. Gronow; Mrs Vaughan (Hillside) and Mrs Capt Stephens.

NEWPORT (PEM.) MEMORIAL HALL.

BALANCE SHEET 1st MAY, 1925, TO 1st MAY, 1926.

RECEIPTS.	£	s	d	PAYMENTS.	£	s	d
Balance in hand from last Account	26	1	10	W. H. James—Lavatories, Door, & Painting ...	18	12	0
Proceeds of Bazaar, per Ladies' Committee ...	65	2	0	O. Davies—Painting Windows, Doors, &c. ...	7	12	0
Per Newport (Pem.) United Choir	20	0	0	Williams & Evans—Electric Current, &c. ...	17	19	6
Per Events Committee	20	0	0	G. Aiken—Additional names on Memorial Tablet	2	10	0
Per Eisteddfod Committee	16	12	9	J. Ll. Havard—Automatic Locks for Lavatories,			
Per Library Committee	9	6	3	&c.	7	0	11
Hire of Hall	12	11	0	J. O. Vaughan & D. Luke—Coal	4	13	5
Donations:—				Claim of Ideal Films, Ltd., & Costs	2	10	3
Capt. and Mrs. Richards, late of Steeple View	5	0	0	Insurance of Hall Building & Contents	3	1	3
Misses James, London	2	2	0	Duck, Son & Pinker—Attending to Piano ...	0	15	6
Mrs. Griffiths, Cardiff (late of Barley Mow)	1	1	0	Cinematograph & Theatre Licences	0	10	0
Mr. Owen Davies, Delfryn	1	0	0	"County Echo"—Printing	1	5	6
Horticultural Society, Newport (Pem.) ...	1	0	0	Brodog Timber Co.—Battens & Carriage ...	0	8	1
Carningli Branch British Legion	0	10	0	Rates	0	18	4
Balance of Fund re Presentation to Mr. E. M.				Jas. Williams & D. Nicholas—Labour	1	3	0
Davies	2	4	0	Adverse Balance of Library Committee, 1925			
Bank Interest on Deposit Account	1	2	3	Account	0	14	8
Sundries	0	1	3	Lloyd's List for 12 months	3	18	0
Balance due to Bank May 1, 1926	1	1	1	E. J. Riley, Ltd.—for Re-covering Billiard Table	13	7	6
				T. W. Evans—Oilcloth for Billiard Room ...	5	12	0
				12 months' Interest on Memorial Hall Debt to			
				1/5/26	37	10	0
				12 months' Interest on Cinema Debt to 1/5/26	4	8	6
				Repayment of capital to Capt. David Owen ...	25	0	0
				Repayment of part Capital to Capt. John Jones	25	0	0
				Cheque Book	0	5	0
	£184	15	5		£184	15	5

Audited and found correct.

E. R. GRONOW & J. I. THOMAS, Auditors.

SUMMARY OF ALL RECEIPTS & PAYMENTS SINCE THE COMMENCEMENT
OF THE ACCOUNT TO 1st MAY, 1926.

RECEIPTS.	£	s	d	PAYMENTS.	£	s	d
From all sources	4099	11	1	Sundry Payments	3845	12	2
Balance due to Bank 1/5/26	1	1	1	Capital Repaid	255	0	0
	£4100	12	2		£4100	12	2

CAPITAL ACCOUNT.

	£	s	d
Amount due on Memorial Hall Mortgage May 1925	750	0	0
Repaid Capt. John Jones 1st May, 1926, £25			
Repaid Capt. David Owen 1st May, 1926, £25			
	50	0	0
	£700	0	0
Amount due on Cinema Account May, 1925 ...	88	10	0
Cancelled by Mrs. Lewis, late of Craigymor, 1st May, 1926	1	0	0
	£87	10	0
Amount due on Capital Account 1st May, 1926 £787	10	0	

D. DAVIES.
J. MILTON DAVIES.
Hon. Treasurers.

DAVID THOMAS, Hon. Secretary.

Audited and found correct.

E. R. GRONOW.
J. I. THOMAS.

May 11th, 1926.

Audited accounts for the Newport Pem. Memorial Hall, 1925-26, part of a document which formed the basis of an agenda for the annual general meeting. This reveals that there were 49 members on the general (men's) committee and the ladies' committee comprised of 77 members. Bear in mind that the population of Newport at this time was just over one thousand and the importance of the Memorial Hall in the life of the community is clear.

The Memorial Hall General Committee, 1923. From left to right, front row: Messrs E.R. Gronow, Tom Williams, David Luke, J.O. Vaughan, F.W. Withington, Sir Marteine Lloyd, Sir George Bowen, Mr Ernest Davies. Second row: Capt Havard, Commodore Van Bowen, Messrs D. Davies, David Rees, Capt Thomas, Messrs J.O. Davies, David Thomas, J. Llewellyn Havard. Back row: Mr J.J. Brown, T.R. Davies, Dewi O. Evans, Willie Lewis, D. Augustus Davies.

Newport Pem. Dramatic Society, 1923. Possibly, the first of their productions presented in the Memorial Hall was *My Lord from Town*. The cast of the play, from left to right, front row: Walter Benson Evans, Doris Davies, Dr David Havard, Dewi Evans, Lillian Evans, Vera Evans and Dick Richards. Back row: D.R. Peregrine, Leila Richards (prompter), Lil Davies, Rene Evans, Gwladys Jones, Arthur Lewis.

Morlais House, West Street, Newport Pem., c. 1938. It was from the garden of these premises that Charles Edwards, the renowned photographer, ran the Newport end of his enterprise. In 1910, the premises were acquired by Mr J.O. Davies who published postcards under the Morlais series. He also conducted business as a newsagent and gents hairdresser. It was in 1937 that the business was taken over by Mr Willie Collings. Mrs Gwladys Collings stands in the doorway.

Spring Hill, Parrog Road, c. 1915. It was in Long Street, a few doors down from The Angel Temperance Hotel that Mr M. Rowlands had his bakery. He also delivered bread and confectionery far and wide using the vehicle shown.

Three
Parrog
the 'other' town

PARROG, NEWPORT PEM.

Parrog Beach, Newport Pem., c. 1910. The Parrog was the main centre for shipping until c. 1930; thereafter it became a playground for children, both old and young.

The Queen's Hotel, Parrog Road, c. 1910. The hotel (first house on the right - now 'Morfan') was one of about twenty-seven public houses in Newport c. 1850. The high tides, which occur at the equinoxes, reach the front of the hotel each year.

Parrog House and the weighbridge, c. 1920. Evidence exists to show that the house was constructed c. 1827. Otherwise, relatively little is known about the property. Traders' vehicles were weighed on the bridge opposite Parrog House both on arrival and departure, and appropriate charges levied.

Approach to Parrog Beach, c. 1908. Behind the doors and the seat was David (Dai) Luke's coal yard. This was but a few yards from the shoreline. To the immediate right of this was one of Newport's three limekilns.

Newport warehouse No 1 (postmarked 1910). At this time, both warehouses were owned by Mr E.J. Griffiths of Trewern. The structure to the left of the building is Newport's second limekiln. Dry bracken and kindling would be placed at the bottom of the kiln, and, thereafter, alternate layers of coal and limestone. The burnt lime would fall through to the base of the kiln before being loaded onto farm wagons and spread over Pembrokeshire's acidic soils.

Shipping at Parrog Beach, c. 1908. The vessel on the right was the *Harparees* which belonged to a Cardiganshire shipowner. She carried culm (a mixture of clay and anthracite dust), and was the only motorised vessel regularly to visit Newport. The other vessel is probably the *Wave* owned by local auctioneer, Mr J.O. Vaughan. The young men are Alan Owen, Ceri Davies and probably two of the Brown brothers - Kenneth and Brynli.

Offloading the ship, Parrog Beach, c. 1912. Sailing vessels would 'park' either side of the river. When the tide had receded, wagons would be drawn alongside, and cargoes offloaded into wagons. On the Traeth Mawr side of the river, it would be necessary to use boards to prevent wagon wheels from sinking in the sand.

Vessel: Le Saviour

Burthen: 6 tons
Crew: 3 men
Master: Henry Roberts
Merchant: Owen Picton
BRISTOL to NEWPORT

16th August 1566	**18th July 1567**	**12th September 1567**
1 t h.h.d. iron	11,000 slate stones	
2 h.h.d. train	(@ 1/8d to 2/8d per 1000)	1 ballet crassum
1 brl tar		2 doz hand cards
2½ t pitch		
½ cwt hops		1 qr hops
½ cwt alum		
1 qr white soap		½ cwt black soap
1 bolt Poldavi		1 bolt Poldavi
1 chest dry wares		
1 fardel linen	1 pack & fardel of frises	
14 bowes		
1 brl teasels		
3 brls salt		3 t salt

Le Saviour was regularly
used to trade with Ireland,
North Wales, and for fishing
in the Severn Estuary

source: Welsh Port Books

Cargo lists of ships visiting Newport Pem., in the 1560s.

Mariners of Newport Pem. (1). Thomas Griffiths was the son of Samuel Griffiths of 'Tyrhos', Mountain Road East. He became a master mariner at the age of 22, and sailed for most of his life with the same chief engineer, William Harries of Kenvor, Dinas Cross. The career of Captain Griffiths was tragically curtailed by an attack of Bright's disease and he died on 27 August 1921 aged 44.

Mariners of Newport Pem. (2). Captain Morris John Morgan married Miss Vera Evans and sailed for many years out of Swansea. He commenced his sailing career c. 1922 and most of his time at sea was spent on the same vessel with his fellow townsman, Mr Richmond Jones (right). Captain Morgan lived at Talar Wen, Feidr Ganol where he is survived by his widow, Vera, now aged 93.

The ferry folk at Newport Pem., c. 1910. Two passengers await the ferry boat on the far side of the river. One of the ferry men in this photograph is thought to be Daniel Mathews. The planks on the front of the boats were placed so that passengers could board the ferry without wetting their feet. In latter years the charge for crossing was one penny at low tide and two pence at high tide.

The ferry folk at Newport Pem., c. 1920. Following the decline of the shipping trade, there were four or five ferry boat owners who were engaged in the business. They included Mr Jack Price, Seagull Cottage; Mr Vince Morris and Mrs Daisy Wylde. Some local octogenarians remember that Thomas John Selby Davies operated his ferry near Riverslee mainly for the use of the golfing fraternity. Mr Jack Price had a habit of wearing several waistcoats so that his money would not rattle, and thus gained himself the nickname of Jack 'No Change'.

Parrog Beach (postmarked 1911). The fact that the tide is low has enabled Mr Rowlands to deliver bread to many houses further down the coast. Seagull Cottage is the white building standing on its own in the centre of the picture.

Promenaders enjoy a walk along the quay wall on Parrog Beach, c. 1910. In the field to the left stands a pole which was widely used for breeches buoy practice, whereby a pulley-mounted cradle large enough to hold a man or woman was moved along a rope secured at two points. This apparatus was widely used for life saving at sea.

Morfa Head from Parrog Beach, c. 1925. Maritime trade was in decline at this time, and this was reflected by the state of the sea defences. These have now been magnificently restored by the Pembrokeshire National Parks Authority.

The *Desdemona*, grounded on Newport Beach in 1906. Official records show that this twin-masted topsail schooner was wrecked on the 'bar' approaches to Newport. The background of the photograph indicates that she was blown on to Traeth Mawr in a north-westerly gale. It is not known whether she became a total wreck or not.

Traeth Mawr, Newport Pem., c. 1955. This was the site once used for the game of 'cnapan'. It is described by the late Revd Evan Jones as one which was 'a mixture of polo and hockey, and was played with a hard wooden ball boiled in tallow to make it slippery. The game consisted of preventing the opposite side from getting the ball over the boundary line. It was thrown or carried by horsemen or footmen. If the horsemen got among the footmen, the latter were allowed to pelt them with stones, this being necessary as the footmen were barefooted. The numbers playing the game amounted to a thousand or fifteen hundred many of whom returned home with bloody noses'.

Young people's visit to Traeth Mawr, c. 1908. It is interesting to note how young people of the period dressed up to go to the beach.

Newport golf links, c. 1960. Although the nine hole golf links was formally opened by Sir Marteine Lloyd on 22 August 1922, only two small buildings were established on the course at that time: a hut where golfers could leave their equipment and another which served as an office for Mr Nurse, the golf professional.

The official opening in 1938 of the club house at Newport Golf Club. Attending the ceremony, from left to right: William Lewis (Barclays Bank); Air Commodore Bowen (Llwyngwair); Mrs Annie Hughes-Rees (schoolteacher); Mrs Evans (Fountain House); Mrs Joyce Joy; -?-; Mr Nurse (the golf professional); Mr J. Bowen Evans. From the doorway (left to right) stand Mr Davies (Cotham Lodge); Mr Tom Thomas (postmaster); Dr Dai Havard and Mr Dan Davies. Others in the group have so far remained unidentified.

Regatta day at Newport Pem., c. 1910. The regatta was originally held near to the warehouse at the Parrog in Newport. This could only take place at high tide. This image by Rita Whitaker RMS delightfully recreates the atmosphere of the event.

Regatta day at Newport Pem., c. 1952. More recently, the regatta has been organised at the Cwm near the Lifeboat House. Judges and referees occupy the larger boat in the centre-ground.

The Lifeboat House, Newport Pem., which was built in 1884. This was established following the wrecking of the Norwegian vessel, *Oline* in 1883. The Revd Evan Jones writes: 'In consequence of this lamentable loss of life (5), a lifeboat was stationed at Newport by the RNLI - one that had been previously presented to the Institution by Mrs Leavington of Clevedon, Somerset... The new boat was launched in the presence of an immense concourse of people, a suitable prayer having been offered up by the writer, a bottle of wine was broken on the boat's bows by Miss Bowen of Llwyngwair, who at the same time named her the "Clevedon".'

The lifeboat ramp at Newport Pem. (postmarked 1906). The lifeboat at Newport, however, could not be launched unless the tide was high; neither could it be launched in a north or the prevailing westerly gale. Its use thus became severely restricted and it was launched only three or so times in the eleven years of its operation. Consequently, the lifeboat station was closed in 1895.

Salmon fishing in the estuary, c. 1910. Over the years, a number of seine nets (known locally as 'y sarn') have been issued to Newport fishermen to fish for salmon and sea trout (sewin). The gentleman on the far right is thought to be Mr Frank Thomas who could reputedly pull the net much harder with his one arm than most men could with two.

The coastline on leaving Parrog, c. 1918. Around the turn of the century, Newport Pem. became a very popular holiday resort with South Wales miners. Pencatman was the headland near the Cwm where they would gather on summer Sunday evenings for their community hymn singing.

Four

Dinas
the community in
between

Greetings card from Dinas Cross (postmarked 1910). Dinas is a long sprawling village which boasts four beaches and a magnificent coastline.

Aberfforest beach and farmhouse, c. 1915. Like most other inlets on the coast, Aberfforest had its own limekiln. At this time, the farmhouse (pictured above) was the home of the Vaughan family in which there were eleven children - ten boys and one girl.

Approach to Cwm yr Eglwys Beach, c. 1912. Probably the most beautiful bay on the North Pembrokeshire coast is that at Cwm yr Eglwys. A number of ships used Dinas as a home port, but only one was built here - a 27 ton sloop named *John* (1928). The extent of the cemetery is worthy of note.

Churchyard and cemetery, Cwm yr Eglwys, c. 1905. The occasion is unknown, but it must have been special to warrant a picture taken by a photographer from Treherbert in the Rhondda!

The 'church remnant' at Cwm yr Eglwys (postmarked 1909). This is all that now remains of the little church established at Cwm yr Eglwys. In October 1859, a terrific storm wreaked havoc and devastation throughout Pembrokeshire, the sea defences and church at Cwm yr Eglwys being among the casualties.

A Sunday school outing (postmarked 1909). Although not much more than a mile from Dinas as the crow flies, the Gwaun Valley might as well be in a different world; for example it is here that the New Year is still celebrated on 13 January. This Jabes Sunday school outing is on its way to Traeth Mawr, Newport, a distance of some six miles. The 'commander of operations' is the Revd J. Llewellyn Morris.

Dyffryn Arms, Gwaun Valley, c. 1955. The Gwaun Valley is well known (or notorious) for its home-brewed beer. The Dyffryn Arms is one of the valley's better known hostelries, where Mrs Bessie Davies still draws beer from a cask and serves it from a jug. It was Mr Jim Jenkins (Jim 'Penrhiw') who walked three miles (each way) to call Dr Dai Havard (see page 63) when Mrs Davies gave birth to one of her four children.

Newport, Dinas and District Celebrities by "Matt."

Some characters from Newport and Dinas, 1935. Many of the characters seen in the photographs and mentioned in the text can be seen in this caricature taken from the *Fishguard County Echo* of 21 November 1935.

Coastguard houses at Dinas Cross, c. 1912. Coastguard stations were dotted along the entire coastline of Pembrokeshire and Dinas, of course, had its own. The first two properties on the right of the picture were houses provided by HM Coastguards for their employees.

An outing from the Glan Hotel, Dinas Cross, 1921. 'Y Gymanfa Fawr' (a large singing festival) was held at Tabor Chapel in 1921 (see page 66a). The staff of the Glan Hotel (above), who provided catering facilities on this occasion, proceed on an outing after feeding the assembled crowd.

The Sailors' Safety Inn, Pwllgwaelod, c. 1930. This lies at the western end of the valley which separates Dinas Island from the mainland, and provided board and sustenance for the many sailors unloading their vessels on the beach.

Sailing vessel at Pwllgwaelod, c. 1910. The beach was used as a discharge point for ships up until c. 1925. Fishguard Harbour is in sight from this point and the *Mauretania* can be seen making one of its regular calls to Fishguard Bay.

Tabor Chapel, Dinas Cross (postmarked 1914). The Baptist movement has always been strong in North Pembrokeshire. Originally local Baptists held their services in private homes or even outdoors, until, in 1792, they secured a piece of land and established the above building. Tabor, Dinas remained a branch of the mother church in Llangloffan until 1799 when it became a chapel in its own right with 103 members. Thomas Griffiths of Trewrach was its first minister.

Aberbach Beach, Dinas Cross, c. 1930. This is a north facing stretch of sand and is the least well known and most secluded of Dinas' four beaches. Pwllgwaelod is about half a mile along the coast to the east.

Five

Fishguard
Lower Town

General view of Lower Fishguard (postmarked 1912). With the establishment of superior harbour facilities at Goodwick, less use was being made of those at Lower Fishguard. Much of the film of Dylan Thomas' *Under Milk Wood* was shot at this location.

Pen Fort, Fishguard

The Fort at Fishguard (postmarked 1917). Several attacks were made by privateers on the town of Fishguard in the latter half of the eighteenth century. The Fort was completed in 1781, in direct response to an appeal from the townsfolk of Fishguard to provide a measure of protection for the town and the shipping which made use of the port facilities at the Lower Town.

R. M. S. "Lusitania" laying off the Fort, Fishguard

The Fort at Fishguard (postmarked 1916) was built at Castle Point (above) on land presented to the town by Gwynne Vaughan of Jordanston. The Privy Council grudgingly approved that eight cannon should be based at the Fort each capable of firing 9 or 12 pound shot.

Shipping at Lower Fishguard, c. 1906. Trade remained brisk throughout the nineteenth century with limestone, culm, coal, timber and manufactured goods being imported. In addition, there were contraband supplies of spirits and wines. Vessels took away with them dairy produce, grain and fish (mainly herring).

FISHGUARD HARBOUR

The herring fleet at Lower Fishguard (postmarked 1907). It is said that the name of the town came from the Nordic 'fis card' meaning 'fish yard'. Indeed, the town became famous for 'sgadan Abergwaun' - Fishguard herrings. Here, four boats of the fleet lie at anchor off the quay wall at what was then still the main harbour for Fishguard.

The quay wall, Lower Fishguard (postmarked 1950). To all intents and purposes, maritime trading at Lower Fishguard ceased at the end of the First World War. Thereafter the occasional ship continued to deliver consignments of flour until c. 1930.

Motor and pleasure boats, Lower Fishguard, c. 1952. By this time, the only craft using the facility were pleasure boats and the fishing boats of the 'lobster-men'. Mr Billy Thomas, now one of the town's undertakers can be seen in the boat in the foreground.

I went here, with Miss B's niece the other day, also to I'd fair we indulged in the horse after two rounds we returned home tired out. love. W.W.

The Gwaun Valley (postmarked 1903). The River Gwaun flows along a glacial valley for a distance of ten miles or so before entering the sea at Fishguard. The Welsh name for Fishguard is Abergwaun - the mouth of the Gwaun river.

Plas Glyn y Mêl, Lower Fishguard, c. 1908. It is said that when the harvests of both land and sea failed (c. 1800), Richard Fenton, eminent historian and nephew of Lieutenant Samuel Fenton arranged for this magnificent mansion to be built in order to provide employment for some inhabitants of the town. He lived here until his death in 1821.

Lower Fishguard, c. 1870. It is interesting to note that the small warehouses at the far end of the quay wall had not yet been built.

The bridge at Lower Fishguard (postmarked 1905). Soon after the top photograph was taken (in 1875) the four-arched bridge was replaced with a single span structure. At one time spring tides regularly flowed over the road at this point.

Warehouse, shipyard and limekiln, Lower Fishguard (postmarked 1908). Joinery workshops, meanwhile, existed in the Slade (centre right) and were used for the repair of ships. Lower Town Hill has proved to be the scene of many road accidents over the years.

HMS *Skirmisher* at Lower Fishguard. To supplement the storage buildings at the end of the quay wall, this very large warehouse was built at the bottom of Lower Town Hill. With the decline of maritime activity in Lower Fishguard, however, the warehouse became redundant. It was subsequently used as a base for a sail training school known as HMS *Skirmisher*.

Fishguard Hill leading to Lower Fishguard (postmarked 1928). The postman delivers his consignment on foot to Lower Town not long after the road on the far bank had been completed in 1923.

Warehouses at Lower Fishguard just before the outbreak of the Second World War. Note the ownership of the warehouses on the quay wall.

Six
Fishguard
Upper Town

Upper Fishguard from the Slade, c. 1912. This is a younger part of the town of Fishguard and was built around the turn of the century. Many more houses have since been added both in the Slade, and along Penslade - the opposite bank. At the end of Penslade was established the Bardic Circle (Y Gorsedd) for the National Eisteddfod of Wales held at Fishguard (Abergwaun) in 1936.

Main Street, Fishguard, c. 1906. Until the arrival of the railway at Goodwick, two horse drawn coaches left the Great Western Hotel daily for the railway station at Haverfordwest - the first at 7.50 a.m. and the second at 4.30 p.m. The journey took about $2\frac{1}{4}$ hours.

Market day, Fishguard Square, c. 1930. Market day is each Thursday, with the bulk of the activity held in the Market Hall - the building on the right underneath the 'herring' weathervane which itself reflects the historical importance of Fishguard as a fishing port.

Fishguard Square (postmarked 1913). Some papers uncovered in the offices of Mr Walter Vaughan (solicitor) revealed that:

'At a meeting held at the Commercial Inn, Fishguard this 4th day of July, 1853 to take into consideration the best means of removing the old garden and premises situate in the centre of the town, which are now a very great nuisance, besides being a great obstruction to all carriages driving into the town, or to the Goodwick road, Mr Colby, the land proprietor having kindly consented to sell the same to the public for the sum of one hundred and twenty pounds of sterling money which, with the cost of transfer and removing the premises may amount to one hundred and fifty pounds.

Present: Mr John Harries, Letterston, Messrs. Thomas Jenkins, Thomas Davies, Levi Vaughan, John Evans, David Vaughan and Thomas Arthur Nicholas. Proposed by Mr Levi Vaughan and seconded by Mr Thomas Davies, that a subscription should be entered into for the purchase, and improvement of the aforesaid nuisance, and that the gentry, land owners, householders, and all persons interested in the trade and property of the town be earnestly solicited to subscribe towards the improvement. It is further proposed by Mr Levi Vaughan and seconded by Mr Thomas Arthur Nicholas, that Mr Wilkins & Co., bankers of Haverfordwest, act as treasurers.'

A list of subscribers attached to the minutes of the meeting suggests that the required amount was readily accumulated. Substantial contributions came from Sir James John and Lady Hamilton (who together gave £20) and from J.H. Phillips MP (£10). Other subscriptions ranged rom £5 to 2s 6d.

Suffragettes at Fishguard Square, c. 1908. Emmeline Pankhurst (above) is seen addressing the crowd assembled on Fishguard Square. The farm machinery 'parked' against the Market Hall is worthy of note as is the probable 'refreshment van' next to the gas lamp post.

St Mary's Church, c. 1916. It occupies a prominent position on Fishguard Square. The Brixham trawlers from Devon often sheltered in Fishguard Bay during a weekend. It is said that the gallery inside the church was reserved on Sabbath mornings for the Brixham fishermen.

Laying of the foundation stone for St Mary's Church Hall, c. 1930. The procession is led by the Revd David Davies BA, BD (Vicar), Haydn Parry (Curate), M.H. Jones and J.R. Richards (church wardens). The Bishop of St David's is also in attendance.

Laying of the foundation stone for St Mary's Church Hall, c. 1930. The hall is situated across the road from the church and its foundation stones were laid by Mrs Mary Louisa Davies of the Vicarage, Fishguard, and by Mrs Beatrice Chambers JP of Plas Glyn y Mêl, Lower Fishguard.

Welsh National Costume

ON THIS BEACH AT 2 O'CLOCK ON 24TH FEBRUARY, 1797, TWO DAYS AFTER LANDING AT CARREG GWASTAD, A FRENCH INVADING FORCE OF 1200 TROOPS COMMANDED BY COLONEL TATE, AN AMERICAN CITIZEN, LAID DOWN THEIR ARMS IN UNCONDITIONAL SURRENDER TO THE 1ST BARON CAWDOR OF CASTLEMARTIN COMMANDING THE FOLLOWING LOCAL UNITS:—

PEMBROKESHIRE YEOMANRY, CARDIGAN MILITIA, FISHGUARD FENCIBLES, PEMBROKE FENCIBLES, NAVAL RATINGS FROM MILFORD HAVEN.

LAST INVASION OF BRITAIN
FISHGUARD, FEBRUARY 1797

Stone at Fishguard Ch

Commemoration French Surrender Goodwick Beach

French Landed Pencaer, Good

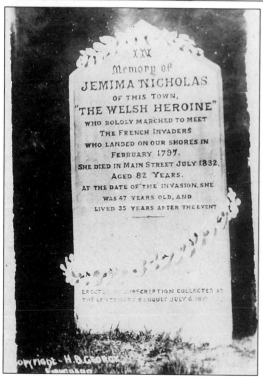

The 'French Invasion of 1797'. One morning in February 1797, three French warships were sighted passing St David's Head, heading north. They put ashore at Pencaer, about one mile west of Fishguard Harbour. For two days, French soldiers drank, ravaged and pillaged local farmhouses. They were eventually persuaded to lay down their arms on Goodwick beach where a plaque is now laid to commemorate the event.

The gravestone of the heroine, Jemima Nicholas. Legend has it that she gathered together the ladies of the town, all dressed in traditional Welsh costume, and that they marched round and round a hill (the Bigney) behind Fishguard. The French were thus deceived into thinking that this was a large military force amassing, and eventually surrendered without a fight.

The Royal Oak at Fishguard Square, c. 1935. It is said that the surrender treaty was signed at the Royal Oak on 22 February 1797. There is some doubt about this, however, since no such document has ever been discovered, only the quill pen with which it was supposedly written.

Brodog Timber Works annual outing (postmarked 1913). The Brodog Timber Works was one of Fishguard's main employers, and was situated at the west end of the town. It remained in operation for about sixty years eventually closing down c. 1965. The outing is on its way to St Davids. Note the solid tyres and chain drive on the vehicle.

High Street, Fishguard, c. 1950. This leads south from Fishguard Square, and formed part of the main A40 road from Fishguard Harbour. The Fishguard County Echo offices were situated on the left hand side whereas the printing works were closer to the Square in a side road called Park y Shut.

Hermon Baptist Chapel, High Street, Fishguard (postmarked 1920). From 1776, the Baptist movement in Fishguard occupied the largest premises available - the Manor House in Fishguard (the Great Western Hotel, see page 76a). It was not until 1832, when these spacious premises were built, that the movement became established in the High Street. It is interesting to note that in 1905, presumably due to the heightened religious enthusiasm during the revival inspired by Evan Roberts, Hermon had 748 members.

Pony and trap in Fishguard High Street, c. 1908. The vehicle stands outside the premises of Furlong's Hackney Carriage Company and is almost certainly one of that company's fleet of vehicles. It was probably used for the carriage, not only of passengers but also of goods.

Furlong's Hackney Carriages, High Street, Fishguard, c. 1908. With the arrival of the railway at Goodwick, there was an increased demand for hackney carriage services. The driver of this 'Phaeton Wagon' was Mr William Lloyd - grandfather of Mrs Katie Evans (née Moon) of Vergam Terrace, Fishguard.

Penslade, Fishguard (postmarked 1906). The message on the card 'hopes that you will get this card as soon as the letter for I have not sent the fish - I will send some up some time again, and don't come to Clarbeston Road for it this time!' (see also page 75).

West Street, Fishguard, c. 1920. This is the main road which leads to Goodwick and the harbour. With the possibility of Fishguard becoming a major transatlantic port, it is not surprising that business premises in this part of town were much sought after.

Brodog Terrace, Fishguard, c. 1908. The Brodog Timber Company established itself at the far end of this terrace of houses. The message reads: 'This is the only bit of fun we had on Christmas Day, and that quite unexpected - don't we look a treat. I hope that you will be able to find us'.

Victoria Avenue, Fishguard, c. 1912. It is interesting to note that while the main road (West Street see page 84b) is made up, the side roads only have very rough surfaces.

Regatta day at Fishguard (postmarked 1906). The regatta was always a major event in the social calendar of Fishguard, and took place between the quay wall at Lower Fishguard and Llanpit Beach. Llanpit was the beach where the town's youngsters took their swimming test, and no-one was allowed to say that they could swim until they had swum from Llanpit to the quay and back at high tide. A rest at the quay wall, however, was permitted.

Regatta day crowds at Fishguard, c. 1906, with everyone suitably dressed for the occasion. The gables on the skyline are those of 'Treforfan' - a large house with a red tiled roof where a group of nuns lived for many years in the 1950s.

Five

Goodwick
the 'twin' town

Goodwick from the Parrog, c. 1920. Fishguard & Goodwick railway station was well established by this time with facilities for handling goods and passengers. A solid tyred 45 hp AEC bus of the Great Western Railway company has collected its consignment of passengers and is bound for Fishguard, Newport and Cardigan.

Fishguard Harbour from the Parrog (postmarked 1916). The Harbour is operational and there is evidence of a ship wrecked on the beach. The peculiar building on the far centre left was the stone crushing plant used in the construction of the Harbour.

Sunday school trip to Goodwick Beach, c. 1909. The unidentified group is posed against the wall to the left of the photograph at the top of this page. A footpath ran alongside the railings allowing pedestrian access to the Fishguard Bay Hotel via the steel bridge.

Main Street, Goodwick, c. 1925. The first building on the right hand side was the police station. This was established at the same time as the Great Western Railway transferred its activities, and workforce, from Neyland to Fishguard.

The road to Harbour Village, c. 1910. The photograph shows that Berachah Chapel has been completed (1906) and otherwise illustrates the narrowness of the road to Harbour Village. The postman delivers his mail to Duke Street - a street which has now been demolished in order to improve access up the hill to Pen Cw.

The Wyncliffe Hotel at Goodwick (postmarked 1905). Wyncliffe House was, for many years, the home of the Rogers family. It was acquired, however, by the Fishguard Bay Railway & Pier Company c. 1896 and subsequently used for meetings between the Company (GWR) and the North Pembrokeshire & Fishguard Railway.

The Wyncliffe as part of Fishguard Bay Hotel (postmarked 1911). In publicity leaflets of 1908 the GWR stated that: 'it was an excellent place to stay en route to or from Ireland.... This pine sheltered hotel is well suited for lovers of wild life - seals and wildfowl abound, and occasionally a rare specimen of the almost extinct wild goat may be seen'.

The Fishguard Bay Hotel (postmarked 1928).

FISHGUARD BAY HOTEL
FISHGUARD, PEMBROKESHIRE.

THE most up-to-date and best furnished Hotel in Wales, with every modern convenience. Ideally situated, overlooking the magnificent Fishguard Harbour and surrounding country. A delightful place to stay at for a Summer or Winter holiday, enjoying remarkable mild and equable climate. Sub-tropical Gardens of great extent and beauty. Close to Harbour where G.W.R. Irish Mail Steamers arrive and leave. Electric Light throughout. Electric Lift to each floor. Telephone in every room for internal communication. Croquet and Lawn Tennis (Hard Court). Eight miles of private Trout Fishing and Deep Sea Fishing. Billiards. Lock-up Garages. Nine-hole Golf Links.

TELEGRAPHIC ADDRESS: Bay Hotel, Goodwick.
TELEPHONE: No. 34 Fishguard.

TARIFFS ON APPLICATION TO RESPECTIVE MANAGERS, OR TO MANAGER, HOTELS DEPARTMENT, PADDINGTON STATION.

Extract from the timetable of the Great Western Railway, 1932.

The funeral of Flight Lieutenant Bush in 1917. During the First World War, a unit of the Royal Naval Air Service (RNAS) was based at Fishguard. Part of their function was to man the aircraft which patrolled the Irish Sea. On 22 April 1917, Flight Lieutenant Bush was involved in a flying accident in which the under carriage of his aircraft caught in the wires from the harbour power house (see page 107a). He died of his injuries three days later.

The funeral of Flight Lieutenant Bush in 1917. He was buried with full military honours and the coffin carriage was escorted by militiamen from the Fishguard Bay Hotel to Fishguard & Goodwick station where the bereaved parents can be seen above.

Fishguard & Goodwick Station (postmarked 1912). The railway finally reached Goodwick in July 1899 over the North Pembrokeshire & Fishguard Railway. This passed through Maenclochog, Rosebush and Puncheston, having left the GWR mainline at Narberth Road (Clynderwen). The approach to Goodwick was through a series of cuttings over a two mile stretch of line and a severe gradient of 1 in 50.

The engine shed at Goodwick, c. 1910. On the right hand side was a standard Churchward two road shed which was opened in 1906. The shed had watering facilities, both at the shed and on the station 'down' platform, a coaling stage, with the usual ramped approach, and a 65 ft turn table, barely visible in the above photograph.

Troops setting up camp in the Marsh Sidings, just below the Bay Hotel, Fishguard. In 1911, dockers in Fishguard felt that they were in a strong position to seek improved pay and conditions. The GWR was most anxious that the Cunard service should not be disrupted in any way and acceded to their request. Only a month after the first stoppage, however, there was a call for a national strike. On this occasion, though, the Fishguard dockers were not successful and soldiers were called in to get the strikers back to work.

Striking dockers at Fishguard, 1913. Two years after the 1911 dispute, harbour personnel were on strike again, and here they can be seen marching from the Bay Hotel.

Goodwick.

Railway approaches to Goodwick, c. 1915. This view shows the nucleus of the town. The importance of the railway is evident from the way in which it dominates the view. Goodwick has a number of 'satellites', namely Dyffryn (in the distance), Stop & Call (up the hill to the right), the Harbour, and, of course, Pen Cw and Harbour Village.

The brickworks at Goodwick which were established c. 1906. A special railway siding was constructed to the works for the transport of raw materials. Goodwick Brickworks became a major employer in the area and continued in operation until the 1960s.

Traffic at Pontiago village, c. 1914, one of a host of villages on Strumble Head.

Strumble Head lighthouse (postmarked 1920). This building, erected c. 1908, replaced another beacon-type structure which had been established on the mainland. This lighthouse, like all others, came under the control of Trinity House. It was manned on a full time basis by a staff of three at any one time - two on the lighthouse and one on leave - until it became automated c. 1980. The term of duty was two months on with one month off.

Eight
Fishguard Harbour

Fishguard Harbour, c. 1950. Sadly, two of the GWR vessels lost in the Second World War were Fishguard based ships - the *St David* and the *St Patrick*. They were replaced by ships of the same name, and the entire fleet can be seen here in the Harbour on a fine summer's day. From left to right: the *St David*, the *Great Western*, the *St Andrew* with the *St Patrick* moored out in the bay.

GREAT BLAST, GOODWICK PIER WORKS, APRIL 19 1905.

To Wish You "A Merry Christmas" from ...

'The instant of the blast', Fishguard Harbour (postmarked 1905). Before the turn of the century, the land on which Fishguard Harbour was built comprised of sheer cliff faces rising to a height of 200 feet. Men had to be lowered on ropes to drill holes in the rock face into which explosives were packed. In all, 2.32 million tons of rock were removed over the next few years.

FISHGUARD-ROSSLARE
shortest sea route to and from SOUTHERN IRELAND
LUXURIOUSLY APPOINTED 54 miles **EXPRESS**
STEAMERS BRITISH RAILWAYS **TRAIN SERVICES**
FACILITIES FOR CONVEYANCE OF MOTOR CARS
Trains run alongside the Steamer at Fishguard Harbour & Rosslare
FURTHER INFORMATION FROM STATIONS OFFICES AND AGENCIES

British Rail poster, Fishguard Harbour, c. 1954. British Railways used their most recent acquisition, the *St David (III)* to promote the service to Rosslare and Southern Ireland, a journey which took about 3¼ hours.

Fishguard Harbour before completion, c. 1905. The original fishermen's quay, which was situated near where the crane can be seen, was replaced by the quay wall as shown. Visible, in the bay, are the Brixham trawlers - frequent visitors to the coast of North Pembrokeshire (see also page 78b).

A view towards the Harbour, c. 1905. Such was the euphoria at Fishguard at this time that photographs were taken and used as Christmas cards. This view from Goodwick Bridge clearly shows the stone crushing plant on the left.

A working crane at Fishguard Harbour, c. 1907. The buildings are taking shape on the quay wall, and work has commenced on the Atlantic Wharf (at the near end of the breakwater). Much work remains to be done on the 2000 ft breakwater. This was laid in 70 ft of water using much of the rock blasted away from the site of the Harbour. John Morris quotes in his book that 'the base width was 300 foot tapering to 70 at the top which was 20 feet above sea level. Every foot of length required 650 tons of stone'.

The building of the inner breakwater, c. 1913. It is suggested that the next development which might have taken place was a cut-off line through Manorowen Wood and over the Drym river. Had this taken place, the Ocean Expresses might have steamed to the end of the inner breakwater. Note the ballast train crossing the bridge over the Parrog.

The men who built the Harbour (postmarked 1906). The Harbour took longer to build than had been anticipated. In all 100 contractors' staff and 400 GWR men were engaged in its construction.

The men who built the Harbour (postmarked 1914). The Harbour became operational at the end of August 1906, but there remained a great deal of work to be done, and gangs of men such as that shown above were engaged on such work until c. 1920.

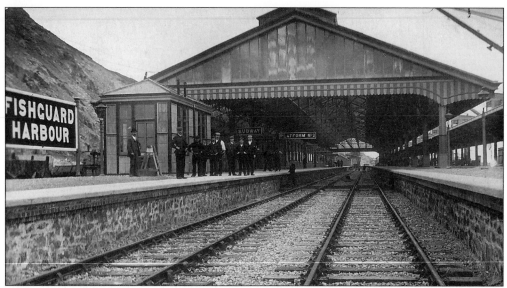

The station canopy viewed from the south (postmarked 1914). The canopy spanned all four platforms at Fishguard Harbour, and the harbourside cranes were pressed into service for lifting the steel trusses into place during its construction. The card shows platforms 2 and 3. Platforms 1 and 2 were mainly used for Ocean Expresses, while No 3 was used only under exceptional circumstances.

The station canopy viewed from the north (postmarked 1908). Fishguard Harbour was described as a 'through terminal'. At the northern end, all lines converged to a single track. This would enable the locomotives of incoming trains to uncouple and run round their trains before proceeding to the engine shed at Fishguard & Goodwick station for servicing. Blocks on the running lines (above) might indicate that this facility was not in use at the time that this picture was taken.

The finishing touches - Fishguard Harbour, 1906. The quay wall is being extended and the crane lowers a concrete block into place whilst other wagons wait to be relieved of their loads. A cattle train waits adjacent to the lairage for its next consignment.

The Harbour nearing operational completion in 1906. A steam crane is used to fill empty wagons with stone and rock, and there is a great deal of 'tidying up' to do near the rock face. It is easy to imagine from this photograph the sheer volume of rock which had to be moved before the Harbour could be built.

Dockers await the next ship, Fishguard Harbour. This card is postmarked 1906 and was printed only one month after the formal opening of the harbour on 30 August that year. The Milford registered tug, *Palmerston*, remains on standby. The power house, with its three chimney stacks, can be seen in the distance while work has yet to commence on the Atlantic Wharf.

Dockside at Fishguard Harbour (postmarked 20 August 1909). Crane details and mountings can be seen much more clearly in this view. Note also the coal wagons in the siding adjacent to the quay wall awaiting loading into the ships.

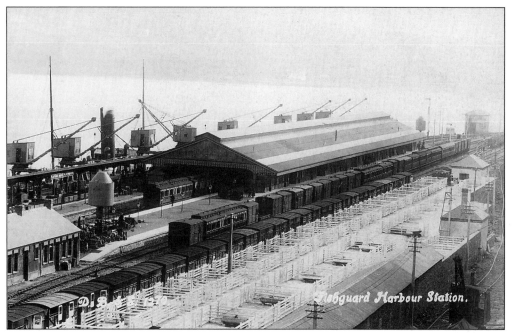

Cattle lairage at Fishguard Harbour, c. 1908. Cattle disembarked at a level below that of the passengers, walked along a ledge built into the quay wall and thence used their own subway to gain access to the lairage above. Passengers thus saw relatively little of the vast cattle traffic from Ireland.

Cattle awaiting rail transport at Fishguard Harbour, c. 1908. The lairage was almost as long as the passenger platforms. Cattle would be inspected by a vet on arrival, and sick animals would be destroyed in an abattoir at the north end of the lairage.

A dredger at work in the Harbour basin, c. 1909. The depth of the water at this point was about 12 fathoms. The harbour authorities however had a perpetual problem of silting which was sufficient to engage a dredger full time. The original dredger, *Agnes*, was lost in a gale in 1901. The replacement, above, was employed thereafter. The silt was loaded into one of two vessels, the *Pioneer* or the *Proteur*, taken out and discharged in the bay.

The Marsh Sidings (postmarked 1909). There was a considerable volume of goods traffic to and from Ireland via Fishguard Harbour. Hand operated points from the down goods loop led to seven sidings with a capability of holding up to 200 wagons, and it was here that most of the shunting was done.

The power house at Fishguard Harbour, c. 1907. Relatively speaking the use of electricity was in its infancy at this time. No expense was to be spared at Fishguard Harbour, however. Electricity was used for lighting and for driving machinery, in particular the cranes on the quay wall (see picture below), and a radio station at Harbour Village.

Offloading the mail at Fishguard Harbour (postmarked 1912). The cranes were used for loading/unloading all manner of goods including motor vehicles. On the quay wall, there was a total of eleven rail-mounted cranes each capable of lifting ten tons, and at the north end of the quay, one fixed crane with a 21 ton capacity.

Harbour Village, Goodwick, c. 1907. The housing stock in Fishguard and Goodwick was not adequate to meet that required when the GWR transferred its activities from Neyland to Fishguard. Coupled with their proposals for the Harbour, therefore, the GWR acquired land overlooking Fishguard Bay where a large number of two and three bedroomed houses were constructed at a cost of up to £175 each.

Harbour Village, Goodwick, c. 1907. In all, the company owned 150 houses in the area although not all were in Harbour Village. Many were built near the railway and engine sheds in Goodwick, for example, St David's Place, where workmen could be called upon at short notice.

Nine

The ferry boats to Ireland

ST. DAVID

FISHGUARD
CROSS
CHANNEL
BOATS
HARBOUR

M.V. INNISFALLEN AND ST. PATRICK

GREAT WESTERN

ST. ANDREW

X.2

The ships which used the Harbour, c. 1950. Up to this time, a comprehensive cross channel ferry service was provided from Fishguard Harbour. There was a daily service to Rosslare provided by ships named after the patron saints. In addition, the *Great Western* sailed on alternate days to Waterford while the Irish owned *Innisfallen* travelled to Cork, also on alternate days.

SS *St George*, c. 1906. This had triple screw turbines and a gross tonnage of 2,456. She was built by Cammell Lairds and arrived at Fishguard Harbour only ten days before the Harbour was formally opened on 30 August 1906. The *St Patrick*, which was built to the same design, by John Brown of Glasgow, arrived later on the same day.

The SS *St David*, which arrived three days later, approaches the quay wall. All these vessels had red funnels with a black band on top, and were registered with the Fishguard and Rosslare Harbours Company. It was two years later that the trio of saints was joined by a fourth sister ship - the SS *St Andrew*.

Cross channel steamers at the quayside (postmarked 27 September 1906, less than a month after the facility had been formally declared open). The message on the card reads: 'The other side shows our new fair station. The Cork boat has two white funnels, Waterford one dark funnel - Rosslare passenger boat two dark funnels…'.

The stokers come up for air, c. 1907. The stokers pose on deck in this photograph by Charles Edwards. The ships at this time were coal fired. This fuel was burnt to raise steam to power the turbine driven propellers.

The SS *Pembroke* is brought alongside, c. 1906. This was one of three vessels brought from New Milford (Neyland) in order to ensure that the daily service to Waterford was maintained at the same level as that which had been run to Neyland. It was on this vessel that the GWR directors made a trial crossing to Rosslare prior to the opening of Fishguard Harbour.

SS *St Julien*, c. 1935. She was a Weymouth based vessel that was often seen in Fishguard on relief duties or when one of the regular vessels was away for overhaul. The *St Julien* survived service as a hospital ship during the Second World War.

A postcard from the Fishguard Route Series (postmarked 1907). Due to the vast expense incurred in building Fishguard Harbour, the GWR were anxious to ensure the success of the project. As part of their marketing strategy, they produced four postcards - the Fishguard Route Series - of which this one shows the *St Patrick* at speed during her sea trials.

Another card in the same series, c. 1907. The slope of the 'gangplank' indicates that the tide was low when the photograph was taken. The 'platform between platforms' was used to assist passengers transferring from boat to train, but could be lowered and tucked underneath the main platforms if there were trains needing to use the track at these locations.

SS *Inniscarra* (postmarked 1913). Ironically, considering the investment in their own boats by the Fishguard and Rosslare Harbours Company, the *Inniscarra* was the first vessel to officially use the newly established port facilities at Fishguard. She, along with all other vessels on this service (except the *Kenmare*), was owned by the City of Cork Steam Packet Company, later the B & I.

SS *Classic* (c. 1912) was one of the vessels which ran on the Cork service in the early days of the Harbour. She belonged to the City of Cork Steam Packet Company and had a gross tonnage of 2,150. It is possible that she was the replacement when the first *Innisfallen* was lost.

114

MV *Innisfallen* (1936). This 'motor vessel' replaced another of the same name which was lost during the First World War. She remained on this service until 1940 when she was replaced for a second time by the *Kenmare*.

SS *Great Southern* (postmarked 1909). This was another of the vessels brought to Fishguard from New Milford. She, too, was engaged on the Fishguard to Waterford service. A clause had been included in the 1898 Act (which incorporated the Fishguard and Rosslare Harbours Company) requiring that the Waterford service be maintained to at least the level appertaining at the time of the Act.

Passengers boarding the ferry at Fishguard (postmarked 1907). All services vied with each other to provide the greatest comfort. Passengers could choose to sail to Rosslare (just under three hours), or to Waterford (about eight hours) or to Cork (about ten hours).

SS *St George*, c. 1914. The outbreak of the First World War represented the beginning of a practice whereby HM Government commandeered the use of non-military vessels for use as part of the war effort. Here we see that the *St George* was pressed into service as a hospital ship.

RMS (Royal Mail Steamer) *St Patrick*, 1935. In 1940 the *St Andrew* and the *St David* were taken over for use as hospital ships. Ironically, it was the *St Patrick*, which remained at its home port that was bombed and sunk off Strumble Head when undertaking a normal service run to Rosslare on 13 June 1941. The master at the time was Captain J. Faraday who had taken his youngest son (home on holiday leave), along with him. Both were lost in the attack.

SS *Great Western*, c. 1946. This ship was built at Cammel Lairds in Birkenhead in 1934, and replaced a vessel of the same name on the Fishguard to Waterford run. She had a gross tonnage of 1,742 and a speed of 14 knots. She could carry 450 passengers with sleeping berths for 85. In the immediate post war years, her master was Captain Baden Mendus.

SS *Kenmare*, seen here c. 1946, had a gross tonnage of about 1,600 tons and was owned by the Coast Lines Company of Ireland. She had a green funnel with black band on top. She served when the first *Innisfallen* was lost in the First World War, and again when the second *Innisfallen* was removed in 1940. She was then in service until the arrival of the third *Innisfallen* in 1948.

A tranquil Fishguard Harbour, c. 1950. With her two sister ships lost (the *St David* at Anzio in 1944, and the *St Patrick* in service off Strumble Head), the *St Andrew* arrives at Fishguard on a fine summer's day whilst *Innisfallen III* is tied up alongside the quay wall awaiting her turn of duty.

Ten

The Cunard era

A poster advertising the Cunard Line, c. 1910. Once the Harbour had been built, Cunard were anxious to announce that passengers en route from America to Europe could save considerable time by disembarking at Fishguard.

The arrival of the *Mauretania* on 30 August 1909. The GWR had been aware of the possibility of attracting Cunard liners before the harbour was built. After years of soliciting the business, the dream became reality with the first visit of the *Mauretania* to Fishguard Harbour exactly three years after the Harbour was formally opened.

The RMS *Mauretania* at Fishguard Harbour where tenders have drawn alongside to take off passengers, luggage and the mails. She had a gross tonnage of 30,704 and a speed of 26 knots. She was the largest and fastest ship afloat in her time and held the 'Blue Ribbon' for the fastest transatlantic crossing from her launch in 1907 up until 1929.

The RMS *Mauretania* gets under way (postmarked 1909). The Mauretania only called at Fishguard on her eastbound journey. Turn-round time at Fishguard was about 45 minutes. In this time, she would discharge, typically, 900 bags of mail and 250 passengers and their luggage.

The RMS *Lusitania* (c. 1910) was the *Mauretania*'s less famous sister. Being built to the same design and degree of opulence as the celebrated *Mauretania* no ship attracted more attention from ship builders and naval architects during her construction. Tragically, she was torpedoed and sunk by a German U-Boat in 1915 with appalling loss of life.

Passengers transfer to the tender in Fishguard Bay (postmarked 1911). In order to further advertise the service, the Great Western Railway produced twenty-four postcards known as the Port of Call series. This was sold for 6d (for all twenty-four) and showed various scenes at Fishguard, in particular the passenger handling associated with the Cunard traffic.

A passenger tender leaves the big ship, c. 1910, and heads for the quay at Fishguard Harbour.

The tender approaches the quay wall at Fishguard Harbour (postmarked 1911). The *Sir Francis Drake* could carry about 250 passengers. Those travelling by rail would be given priority, rushed through customs, and thence to catch trains which would whisk them off to Cardiff, Paddington and beyond.

The party at Fishguard Harbour, 30 August 1909, gathered to welcome the disembarking passengers.

The Ocean Express, seen here leaving Fishguard Harbour c. 1912, required two engines of the Flower class to help it overcome the very steep bank out of Fishguard. During the course of its five hour journey to Paddington, this train would make one stop only, at Cardiff, where passengers' mail was dropped and a change of engines was made.

The dining saloon on the Ocean Express, c. 1912. The GWR spared no expense in promoting the Cunard traffic. Here another card from the Port of Call series highlights the standard of the dining cars on these trains.

An Ocean Express leaves the Harbour on 30 August 1909 drawn by No 4116 Mignonette and No 4111 Anenome. A typical train would comprise of ten vehicles of bogie stock, including mail and luggage vans and restaurant cars - a full loading of about 310 tons.

An Ocean Express rushes through Fishguard & Goodwick station, on 'Mauretania Day', 30 August 1909. The excitement at Fishguard at this time could scarcely be contained. Crowds line the platform at the station to cheer the train through and the people of Fishguard stroll along the Parrog in a continuous column; even a fun fair has been brought in for the occasion.

The RMS *Aquitania* was the largest vessel to visit Fishguard Harbour. She was built in 1914 and listed as 45,647 tons gross. She had an operational speed of 23 knots and was just over 900 feet long. This photograph by Charles Edwards shows her in Fishguard Bay.

The opulence of the *Aquitania*, c. 1917. It was said at the time that 'her great dimensions have rendered possible public rooms of such proportions and such perfection of architectural arrangement and decorative art as mark an advance even upon the elegance of the *Mauretania*, and this is by no means limited to the accommodation provided for first class passengers, but extends throughout second and third class quarters'.

The tug *Frank*, one of the support vessels at Fishguard, c. 1909. Although the larger Cunarders did not enter inside the north breakwater at Fishguard, it was still necessary to be able to turn them prior to their onward journey to Liverpool and *Frank* was engaged for this purpose.

The tender SS *Atlanta* (postmarked 1912). With Cunarders calling at Fishguard every ten days or so, many of the support vessels were idle for much of the time. During this 'unproductive' period, the GWR often ran pleasure trips up the coast and here we see one such trip with the SS *Atlanta* calling at New Quay.

Blue Funnel Line SS *Aeneas* at Fishguard Harbour, 1910. It was thought and hoped that, with the transatlantic traffic calling, the port would be further developed. Indeed, use was made of Fishguard as early as 1908 by both the Booth and Blue Funnel lines. However, with increasing competition from other ports, and the outbreak of the First World War, the dream was sadly not to be fully realised.

Acknowledgements

Several local organisations appear to have enjoyed the talks that I have given when presenting my collection of postcards, photographs and ephemera of this area. The enjoyment has undoubtedly been enhanced by the historical sketches and anecdotes used both to amplify the presentations and as captions here in this book. I must confess that I have relied heavily on the memories of many of my fellow townsfolk, and in this regard, I must record my thanks to Mrs S. Crocker, Mr Peter George, Mr Will Harries, Revd A.W.R. Hughes (Aberystwyth), Revd Robbie Jones, former Chief Inspector Winston Jones, Mrs Joyce Joy, Mr David Lewis, Mr Mervyn Phillips, Mr Glan Rees, Mr and Mrs Vivian Roberts and Mr Ken Williams.

I would like to express my gratitude to Sir Lincoln Hallinan for contributing an excellent, thoughtful foreword to this book.

I am indebted to Mrs Rita Whitaker; the National Library of Wales, and Studio Jon for permission to print some of the plates.

Mrs Enid Davies and Mrs Vera Morgan have been particularly helpful and I would like to thank them warmly for their researches, generosity, and tolerance of my incessant questioning.

I am particularly indebted to Mrs Kathy Phillips for her tireless efforts to secure and select suitable material for this book, and for assistance with writing and scrutinising the script.

There have been times when the going has got tough. At such times, I have been able to call upon the assistance of Mr Simon Eckley of The Chalford Publishing Company who has always given me encouragement and constructive comment.

I must, however, reserve the warmest thanks for my mother, Mrs Lit Lewis, whose enthusiasm for my hobby has been a constant source of inspiration. Without her memory to rely on, it is likely that the book would not have seen the light of day.